Kids' **TRAVEL GUIDE** to the **Beatitudes**

REPRODUCIBLE TS INCLUDED!

Group
Loveland, Colorado
group.com

Group resources really work!

This Group resource incorporates our R.E.A.L. approach to ministry. It reinforces a growing friendship with Jesus, encourages long-term learning, and results in life transformation, because it's

Relational
Learner-to-learner interaction enhances learning and builds Christian friendships.

Experiential
What learners experience through discussion and action sticks with them up to 9 times longer than what they simply hear or read.

Applicable
The aim of Christian education is to equip learners to be both hearers and doers of God's Word.

Learner-based
Learners understand and retain more when the learning process takes into consideration how they learn best.

Kids' Travel Guide to the Beatitudes

Copyright © 2013 Group Publishing, Inc. / 0000 0001 0362 4853

Visit our website: **group.com**

Credits
Chief Creative Officer: Joani Schultz
Executive Editor: Christine Yount Jones
Editor: Jennifer Hooks
Assistant Editor: Becky Helzer
Contributing Authors: Anne Bosarge, Danielle Christy, Rhonda Haslett, Amy Nappa, Siv Ricketts, Larry Shallenberger, Emily Snider, Sophia Winter, Henry Zonio
Art Team: Jean Bruns, Suzi Jensen, RoseAnne Sather
Cover Artist: Drew Hill
Illustrations: Ed Koehler

ISBN 978-1-4707-0423-0

10 9 8   22 21 20 19

Printed in the United States of America.

Table of Contents

Kids' Travel Guide

An Introduction to the Travel Guide

The Sermon on the Mount is one of the most enduring, beloved moments in Jesus' earthly ministry. Jesus singlehandedly revolutionized how people viewed God and their relationship with him. On the hillside that day, Jesus made the radical statement that our good deeds won't earn us eternal favor with God—contrary to the popular teaching of the day. Instead, Jesus said, it's our internal transformation that results from our faith that matters to God. Listening to Jesus' teaching, deepening our personal relationship with God, and letting our love for Jesus shine through our behavior and actions—that's what matters. In that time, this was revolutionary teaching. And people from far away flocked to listen to Jesus' astonishing words.

Jesus' message in the Beatitudes is especially poignant today. Kids face struggles every day. Whether it's trying to understand why they're in trouble for standing up for what they think is right or coping with a schoolyard bully, Jesus' words in the Beatitudes ring especially true today for the youngest of our faith. Jesus' message holds the same profound and assuring appeal for kids as for adults; his words are words to live by for the faithful looking for transformation, comfort, assurance, and strengthened faith.

As you travel through the Beatitudes, invite kids to journey with you to the hillside where Jesus sat long ago and taught the masses. Like the Bible words themselves, the 13 journeys in this book will surprise, comfort, and challenge your children.

Kids' Travel Guide to the Beatitudes is designed to be applicable to kids ages kindergarten through fifth grade. The lessons explore 13 truths of the Beatitudes, each imparting deeper understanding and reliance on God.

During this 13-week journey, each child will complete a **Travel Journal.** The Travel Journal will serve as a keepsake so kids can continue to remember the concepts of the Beatitudes.

The **Pathway Point** is the central concept that children will explore and apply to their lives. The **In-Focus Verse** spotlights the specific verse the lesson explores. A **Travel Itinerary** introduces the lesson and explains how the lesson will impact children's lives.

Please read each lesson thoroughly, and make a model for the crafts before your lesson. If you do, your lessons will flow much more smoothly. The time recommendations are only guidelines. They'll change according to how many are

in your group, how prepared you are, and how much help you have. Choose activities or adapt them based on the size of your group and the time you have during your class.

Each lesson starts with a **Departure Prayer**. These are creative prayer activities that help introduce the topic and focus children on God. **Tour Guide Tips** are helps for the teacher, and **Scenic Routes** provide additional creative options.

First Stop Discoveries introduce the children to the lesson's topic. The **Story Excursions** dive deeper into the Beatitude. Kids will experience the Bible in creative and varied ways. Choose what you think will best meet your children's needs. The activities in **Adventures in Growing** lead the children into further application of the Pathway Point. Each week, ask the children if they had opportunities to demonstrate the previous week's Pathway Point in their lives. This will be an important faith-growing time.

Souvenirs include paper activities at the end of the lessons to copy for each of the kids in your group. Have children collect these and keep them in their Travel Journal. When your study on the Beatitudes is complete, each child will have a keepsake to use as a reminder of all he or she has learned. Each lesson closes with a **Home Again Prayer**, which offers a time of commitment and a time to ask God to direct kids' lives.

Anytime during your lesson, read the **Fun Facts** section to the kids. These provide examples of the lesson's point with familiar and not-so-familiar facts.

May this exploration of Jesus' important teachings in the Beatitudes bring you and your children to a deeper realization of God's great love for you.

JOURNEY 1

Jesus Calls His Disciples

Pathway Point: Jesus wants to be our friend.

Scripture: Matthew 4:18-22

In-Focus Verse: "Jesus called out to them, 'Come, follow me, and I will show you how to fish for people' " (Matthew 4:19).

Travel Itinerary

This account of Jesus calling his disciples is abbreviated (Luke and John's Gospels provide much more detail), but still captures just how much Jesus values human relationships and how he wants to be in relationship with his people. We see Jesus personally recruiting people to be his disciples, which was an unheard-of practice for a Jewish rabbi. It was typical for a rabbi to be approached—not to approach. But Jesus takes the initiative and goes to the shores of Galilee and recruits—you got it—*commercial fishermen*. He first recruits a pair of brothers, Simon and Andrew. And Jesus' pitch to them is quite unique. He invites them to become his disciples and promises that in turn, he'll show them "how to fish for people."

Those words must've been puzzling to the disciples because such a promise was attributed to God as a signal that the Messianic Age—the time of the Messiah—was at hand. These rough fishermen didn't know exactly what Jesus had in mind—but they knew enough to realize that Jesus was inviting them to be a part of something big. The fact that they followed him confirms that Jesus successfully baited their imaginations.

The action continues with Jesus, Simon, and Andrew coming upon another set of sibling fishermen, James and John. It's likely that the two sets of brothers already knew one another since they shared a common vocation and lake. Jesus worked through these pre-existing relationships to invite the men to follow him and to be his friends.

This history is important because it reminds us of two important truths. One, Jesus works through existing friendships to build new friendships with him. And two, his charge to the disciples to become fishers of people reminds us that Jesus wants to be friends with each of us.

> **TOUR GUIDE TIP**
>
> The experiences in this book have been designed for multi-age groups. Select from the experiences, or adapt them as needed for your kids.

Items to Pack:

1 sturdy blanket per 4 people

(up to 5 minutes)

This "fishy" prayer will get your children thinking about the best part of being Jesus' friend.

Gather kids around you and say: **Today we're going to be looking at an event in the Bible that tells us Jesus wants to be our friend. Here's what happened: Jesus met a group of people who caught fish by tossing large nets into the water—they were fishermen. Jesus wants to be our friend, so he invited his new friends to help him. He taught them how to become fishers of people so that even today, Jesus could make new friends when people get to know him.**

Let's pretend to be fishermen and cast nets while we thank Jesus for wanting to be our friend, too. Give a blanket to every four children. Show kids how to work together to cast their blanket by tossing it while holding onto one corner.

Say: **Now take turns casting your net. After you cast your net, pray to Jesus by finishing this sentence: "Dear Jesus, the best part about you wanting to be my friend is _____."**

Encourage all kids to take a turn casting their net and praying.

When everyone's finished, pray: **Jesus, thank you for wanting to be our friend. Help us learn ways to introduce our friends to you. In your name, amen.**

(15 minutes)

Make New Friends

Kids discover that making new friends is easier than they think.

Say: **Jesus wants all his friends—us included—to invite new people to become friends with him. Jesus loves everyone and wants to be their friend. He wants people who love and follow him to share him with friends. Let's take a moment and remember what it's like to make a new friend.**

Ask: **• Tell about a time you were in a room with a bunch of other kids and you didn't know anybody.**

• When you're in a situation where you don't know others, what's it like to introduce yourself to someone new?

• **Describe how you introduce yourself to someone new. What kinds of things do you do when you want to meet a new friend?**

Say: **Those are great ideas. Here are more things you can do to make new friends.**

First, smile. Smiling is a great way to show that you're happy and friendly. It also lets other people see you're happy to meet them.

Turn to a partner and show your best smile. Pause. **Now turn to someone else and show your smile.** Pause.

There's nothing better than a good smile. In fact, scientists tell us that smiling releases chemicals in our body that make us feel good. Looking at someone else's smile has the same effect. So when you smile at someone who looks like he or she needs a friend, you're signaling that you're a friendly person.

The second thing you can do is shake hands. This is another way to be friendly and let people know you're happy to meet them. When you shake someone's hand, offer the person your hand, take his or hers, and pump it two or three times. Let's try that, combined with the first skill—smiling. Find someone and give that person a big smile and then shake hands. Do that with three different people.

The last thing you can do is share your name. That's as easy as saying, "Hi! My name is _____. What's yours?" Pause.

Let's put these three friend-making skills together. Walk around our room and "meet" three new people. If you already know everyone, that's okay—go and pretend to introduce yourself to three different kids. Remember: Give each person a big smile, shake hands, and tell each other your names. Allow time for kids to do introductions.

Ask: • **Explain what you were thinking as you introduced yourself to others.**

• **What did you discover about making introductions?**

Say: **The last step to making new friends is the most fun: It's finding out what you have in common. Let's form groups of three.** Once kids are in groups, take a poll:

Raise your hand if you like pizza.

Raise your hand if chocolate is your favorite flavor of ice cream.

Raise your hand if you have a brother or sister.

Say: **Wow—I saw a lot of hands. I'm sure lots of you already found one thing you all have in common. Now for the challenge: Let's see**

Flashing a toothy smile not only helps you feel good—it's also good for your health. Research shows that smiling relaxes the human body and helps reduce stress. Smiling also helps make your immune system work better. And smiling also produces natural painkillers called endorphins and other chemicals that help people feel better.

Handshaking has been around since the days of the ancient Greeks. Nobody's pinpointed why it started, but some people believe that since soldiers held their weapons in their right hand, shaking hands was a sign of friendship and showed a soldier was unarmed and came in peace.

TOUR GUIDE TIP

If groups finish early, let them keep talking. One of the benefits of Christian education is creating environments where kids can build Christian friendships with peers.

TOUR GUIDE TIP

Church is an excellent place for children to make new friends. Help kids practice the skills they just learned in your ministry. Encourage kids to introduce themselves to new kids and to play the "What Do We Have in Common?" game with peers at school. Affirm children whenever you see them being friendly to new kids to reinforce this friend-making behavior.

just how much you have in common. When I say "Go!" your group must find 10 things that all of you have in common. It might be foods you all like to eat, TV shows you all like to watch, music you all like to listen to, or books you all like to read. It could be anything!

Ready? Go!

Give groups time to find 10 things in common. Encourage kids to keep count of their common traits with their fingers.

When time's up, bring groups together and ask:

• **What surprising things did you discover everyone in your group had in common?**

• **What made it easy or difficult to find things you *all* had in common?**

• **How could this game help you make new friends?**

• **You learned a lot of details about each other in this game. Why do you think Jesus wants to know details about our lives?**

Say: **It's fun to make new friends. But we can feel nervous or shy when we meet new people. We don't need to feel that way. Most people like to make new friends. That's how God made people. The Bible says 🌑 Jesus wants to be our friend. He wants us to make new friends, too. This way, more and more people can learn about Jesus through us and become friends with him. So don't be afraid or shy! Take a chance and make new friends using your new skills.**

Ask: • **Describe a place you might meet new kids you could make friends with.**

• **Tell about a situation where someone took the time to be your friend.**

• **Why do you think God designed us to have friends?**

Say: **Jesus wants us to follow his example and make new friends. Jesus loves everyone. 🌑 Jesus wants to be our friend. So let's make an effort to make new friends and help them get to know how great it is to be friends with Jesus.**

(up to 10 minutes)

Let's Go Fishing

This hands-on experience lets kids imagine what it was like to be an early-century fisherman and discover what Jesus meant with his unusual invitation to become "fishers of people."

Items to Pack:
blankets from the previous experience

Say: **Now that we've learned a little about making friends, let's look at a time in the Bible where Jesus made new friends and invited them to follow him.**

Open your Bible to Matthew 4:18-22, and show kids the passage in the Bible.

Say: **In Jesus' day, lots of people fished on the Sea of Galilee.**

Ask: • **Tell about a time you went fishing.**

• **What do you have to do to get ready to go fishing?**

• **Explain what you need to do to successfully catch fish.**

Say: **When we go fishing, we use fishing poles and hooks to catch fish. But these fishermen needed to catch a lot of fish to make a living. They wouldn't have been happy to go home at the end of the day with a small bucket of fish. They needed to catch dozens and dozens of fish so they could sell them at the market to make money to feed themselves and make a living.**

So the first thing they did when they went fishing was to row their boats out to the middle of the water where the fish swam in big schools.

Have kids form groups of four, and give each group a blanket. Explain that each group is a fishing crew. Have them stand in formation and pretend to row their boat out into the deep water by standing in a line and rowing together as they walk together toward the middle of the room.

Next they would cast their nets into the water.

Have children work together to cast their blanket nets into the water.

And they'd wait until their nets were full of fish and then pull them back in.

Have children pretend to haul their nets filled with fish back in.

Then they would move their boats to a different part of the lake...

Have children "row" their boats to another part of the room.

And cast their nets again.

Have children pretend to cast their nets.

When the nets were full of fish again, they'd pull the new catch into the boat.

Have children pretend to pull their heavy nets filled with fish back into the boats.

At the end of the day they'd row back to shore.

Have children row their boats back to shore where they started.

And they'd load their fish into carts so they could take them to market to sell.

Have children pretend to pick up their fish and place them into a cart.

Finally, they'd inspect their fishing nets and look for holes. Whenever they found a hole, they had to repair the rope so fish wouldn't get away the next time they went fishing.

Have children pretend to tie knots in broken pieces of rope.

Ask: • **What skills do you think fishermen might need to learn to do their job well?**

• **Explain how long you think it took someone to learn how to become a fisherman.**

Say: **These fishermen were serious. Fishing was the family business. Their fathers were fishermen. And these men probably expected to have their own families someday and pass the fishing business to their children as well. But then something happened. A man named Jesus came to visit them and changed all their plans.**

One day, Jesus visited the fishermen Simon and Andrew and invited them to become his friends. Jesus wanted them to follow him and learn how to live in a way that honored God. Jesus wants to be our friend, and he wanted to be their friend, too.

The Bible tells us that Jesus said something odd to the fishermen Simon and Andrew. He told them he'd make them "fishers of people." They knew how to catch fish—but people?

Ask: • **What do you think it means to become fishers of people?**

• **Why do you think Jesus cared about fishing for people?**

Say: **Jesus' words must have been confusing for Simon and Andrew. But Jesus wasn't talking about capturing people in nets. He was using a word picture to say something very important. He was telling Simon and Andrew that if they became his friends and came with him, he'd teach them how to gather lots and lots of people and introduce them to Jesus. They would have a very important purpose.**

Ask: • **Describe what kinds of skills you think people would need to become fishers of people.**

FUN FACT The most common fish found in the Sea of Galilee is the sardine. So chances are Simon, Andrew, John, and James used their nets to pull in hundreds and hundreds of those tiny fish.

• **If you had the opportunity, explain whether you'd choose to follow Jesus and become a fisher of people, or stay with the fishing job you already knew.**

Say: **The Bible says Simon and Andrew decided to accept Jesus' offer and become fishers of people. This made Jesus happy because** 🐟 **Jesus wants to be our friend. He was happy to have people who wanted to help others learn about him.**

Jesus and his two new friends walked down the shore and met two more brothers who were fishermen, John and James. Jesus offered the same invitation to these brothers, and they, too, left their nets and became friends and followers of Jesus.

🐟 **Jesus wants to be our friend, and he wants us to help new people learn about him.**

<table>
<tr><td>ADVENTURES IN GROWING</td><td>

(up to 15 minutes)

Go Fish

This healthy snack will energize your kids and give them a chance to discuss what they've learned about Jesus wanting to be our friend.
</td></tr>
</table>

Beforehand, prepare the whipped cream cheese by adding several drops of blue food coloring into the container and stirring it.

Have kids wash their hands or use an antibacterial hand wash to clean up before handling food. Distribute the plates, napkins, and plastic knives.

Give each child a napkin with a rice cake on it and about a spoonful of cream cheese. Show kids how to spread the cream cheese on their rice cake to represent the surface of a lake. Have them place a few fish-shaped crackers on the water to represent the fish that Simon, Andrew, James, and John caught. Distribute cups with water or juice.

Before kids eat, pray: **Dear God, we thank you that** 🐟 **Jesus wants to be our friend. Help us become fishers of people, too. Thank you for this snack. In Jesus' name, amen.**

As kids eat, ask: • **Tell about a time you introduced a friend to Jesus.**

• **Why do you think Jesus wants to be our friend?**

• **What's important about being Jesus' friend?**

Say: **When Simon, Andrew, James, and John sat down at the end of that day, they must have been completely amazed. They woke up as fishermen, doing what they'd always done. By the end of that day,**

Items to Pack:

rice cakes, whipped cream cheese, blue food coloring, fish-shaped crackers, small bowl, plates, plastic knives, napkins, disposable cups, water or juice to drink.

ALLERGY ALERT ▸ Check with parents about allergies and dietary concerns, and post a copy of the "Allergy Alert" sign (at the end of this book) where parents will see it.

Parents, we will be eating a snack in class today. Please let your child's teacher know if your child has any allergies or dietary concerns.

ALLERGY

We're serving...

ALERT!

TOUR GUIDE TIP

A small percentage of children have lactose intolerance or dairy allergies and won't be able to enjoy the cream cheese. If you have a child who can't eat dairy, substitute cream cheese with a non-dairy can of blue frosting.

though, they had a new job—they were fishers of people. And they'd made a new friend in Jesus.

The best part of this passage is that it reminds us 🌏 **Jesus wants to be our friend. Jesus wants to be friends with everyone we know, too. Let's play a game to learn more.**

Have children sit in a circle. Give each child another napkin. Set the bowl of fish-shaped crackers in the middle of the circle and say: **Tell about the members of your family.** Allow time for kids to describe their family's makeup.

Say: **Jesus wants to be friends with everyone in your family. So let's pass around the bowl and you can each take one cracker for each member of your family and set the crackers on your napkin.** Pause.

Now think of three of your close friends. Tell someone next to you the names of those friends. Pause.

Now take three fish, one for each good friend. Pause.

Jesus wants to be friends with your good friends, too!

Finally, think of the person you have the hardest time getting along with—maybe a brother or sister or someone at school who bullies you. Once you have that person in mind, write his or her name on the floor in front of you with your finger. Pause.

Guess what? Jesus knows all the bad things this person has done to you and all the ways you struggle to get along—and he still wants to be that person's friend. The truth is that _all_ of us, including the person whose name you wrote, do things that are wrong. Even though Jesus knows this about us, 🌏 **Jesus still wants to be our friend.**

It's amazing that Jesus wants us to fish for all kinds of people to be his friends. He wants us to help him befriend people who do good things and people who do wrong things. It doesn't matter to him. He has the power to forgive anybody's sin. 🌏 **Jesus wants to be our friend.** Let kids eat their crackers and enjoy a drink.

Items to Pack:
Bibles, 1 copy per 3 kids of the "Friends With Jesus" handout (at the end of this lesson), pocket folders, pens, solid paint color sample strips in shades of blue (available at paint and hardware stores), fish stickers (available at craft stores), hole punches, scissors, ribbon, markers

> **SOUVENIRS** →

(up to 20 minutes)
A Net Full of Friends

This activity will get your children working independently and in groups to explore other examples in the Bible where Jesus made friends with all kinds of people.

Beforehand, cut one 8-inch piece of ribbon per child. Cut a few extras for guests.

Set out markers and distribute one pocket folder to each child. Have kids write their names on the front. The folders will serve as kids' Travel Journals to collect the Souvenir experience in each lesson. Kids will take their Travel Journals and souvenirs home after Lesson 13 to remind them of Jesus' Sermon on the Mount and the Beatitudes.

Have children form trios, and give each group a Bible.

Say: **Imagine if we could find other examples in the Bible where Jesus went out of his way to make friends with someone new. This would be a way to be extra sure that** **Jesus wants to be our friend.**

Each group will get a handout with a Bible verse circled on it. Together, look up and read the circled passage and then discuss the questions at the bottom of the page. When you've finished, work as a team to figure out how you'll act out the passage. You can do a short play or pantomime or whatever you can think of. Your job is to present the story so everyone can learn about the passage you just studied.

Give each group a copy of the "Friends With Jesus" handout, with a different Bible passage circled on each copy. If you have a larger group, assign a few of the groups the same passage. Give groups about 10 minutes to work. When they all finish, have them return to the large group. Give each group a chance to act out what happened.

Ask: • **What's the same about how Jesus treated every new friend he met?**

• **What, if any, differences did you notice among the passages?**

• **Explain why you think Jesus chose to make friends with people most others ignored.**

Say: **The four Gospels—the collections of writings about Jesus—are full of examples of Jesus meeting new friends and the loving and kind way he treated those people. That's because Jesus loves everyone. Every person is very special to Jesus. That's why** **Jesus wants to be our friend—no matter who we are or what we've done.**

Our very first journey into the part of the Bible we call the Beatitudes might be our most important one, because it helps us understand _why_ Jesus gave this important message that day. He spoke out of love for them and for all of us. Since we know **Jesus wants to be our friend, we can have faith that everything he said is true.**

Let's make a souvenir to remind us of the awesome fact that **Jesus wants to be our friend.**

Give each child a blue paint sample strip, several fish stickers, and an 8-inch piece of ribbon.

Say: **We're going to make bookmarks. First, take turns using the hole punch to make a hole near the top edge of your paint-strip lake.** Allow time.

The different shades of blue are like the waves that the fishermen in our Bible passage bobbed up and down on. Go ahead and add fish stickers to your lakes. Allow time.

Now write today's Pathway Point on your bookmark. Write "Jesus wants to be our friend." Allow time.

Almost done. Next, we're going to make a tassel for our bookmark. Take your piece of ribbon and fold it in half by touching the ends together. Pinch the ribbon together just below the halfway point. See the little loop that makes? Push the loop through the hole you punched in your bookmark. Allow time.

Now grab the two ends of your ribbon and thread them through that loop. Allow time.

Now pull the ends of the ribbon tight until the loop wraps tight around the bookmark. Allow time.

You did it! Now place your bookmark in your folder. This is your first souvenir from our journey. When we complete our final journey, you'll get your folder filled with all the souvenirs we make together. This one will help you remember that **Jesus wants to be our friend.**
Collect the Travel Journals, and put them away till next week.

Items to Pack:
blankets from the previous experiences

HOME AGAIN PRAYER	(up to 5 minutes)

Form groups of four and give each group a blanket. Have the groups each stand in an imaginary boat. Say: **Let's use our blankets one more time to remember what we've learned today. Simon, Andrew, James, and John were fishermen.**

Have kids work together to cast out their blanket nets.

They were highly trained at catching fish.

Have kids work together to pull fish back into the boat.

But Jesus caught them with his love and friendship.

Have kids work together to cast out their nets again.

And Jesus invited the disciples to help him catch more new friends.

Have kids work together to pull their nets back into the boat. Say: **Now huddle close together and wrap the blanket around you like it's a great big hug.** Allow time. **Now repeat this prayer after me:**

Dear Jesus (pause),

Thank you for loving everyone (pause)

And wanting to be our friend (pause).

We love you and want to be your friend, too (pause).

We want to become people who share you with our friends (pause).

In your name, amen.

Say: **Now give each other a great big hug as a way to remind each other that** ● **Jesus loves you and wants to be your friend.**

Friends With JESUS

Directions:

On this page you'll find a circled Bible reference that tells about a time Jesus made a new friend. Together with your group, look up and read the Bible passage. Discuss the questions at the bottom of the page, and then work together to act out the passage.

Luke 19:1-10   John 1:41-51

John 4:4-13

Matthew 9:9-13   John 3:1-21

Things to Discuss:

- Tell about the person Jesus met in your Bible passage. What characteristics did you notice about that person?

- Describe how Jesus befriended the person.

- In this example, what can you learn from Jesus about making friends with others?

The Crowds Follow Jesus

Pathway Point: We want to follow Jesus.

Scripture: Matthew 4:23-25

In-Focus Verse: "Large crowds followed him wherever he went—people from Galilee, the Ten Towns, Jerusalem, from all over Judea, and from east of the Jordan River" (Matthew 4:25).

Travel Itinerary

After Jesus partially built his team of 12 followers (Matthew didn't join up with Jesus until later), he began his public ministry of teaching and preaching throughout Galilee. Matthew summarized the content of Jesus' message by calling it "the Gospel of the Kingdom." Jesus was ushering in the rightful rule of God, and he was inviting everyone to become citizens of God's good reign. Jesus moved throughout Galilee and preached in the synagogues at each city he visited. Several of the Old Testament prophets prophesied that God would send the Messiah ("The Chosen One") to announce and establish God's kingdom. Isaiah gave some very detailed information about what this "chosen one" would be like and declared that one of the signs that the time of Messiah was coming to pass was that he would heal people of their sickness and diseases (Isaiah 35:5-6, 53:5).

Naturally, the public's reaction to Jesus' ministry was overwhelming. Families and friends brought their sick ones to Jesus with hopes that he would heal them. Matthew makes note of the most intense cases—epileptics, demonic possessions, and paralytics. And Jesus didn't disappoint. "He healed them all," Matthew wrote.

Jesus' teaching and healing created an immense stir throughout the region. Matthew 25 offers a geographical description that shows Jesus drew crowds of curious and expectant followers from all over Israel. People came from the urban centers (the Ten Towns) and from the more rural areas (Galilee), and from both sides of the Jordan River to experience Jesus for themselves.

The Israelites were hungry for God's kingdom to come. As a consequence of violating their covenant with God, they'd been carried off into exile in Babylon for decades. However, there was no immediate sense that God's rule had been restored. Israel was invaded first by the Greeks and later by the harsh Roman armies, and they continued to languish under cruel occupation at the time of Jesus' birth. Jesus' words and actions sparked hope in the hearts of the masses.

Certainly many who came out to see Jesus did so for the practical reason of having their loved ones made whole. But many must have been considering whether they would put their trust in this upstart preacher and actually follow him.

This passage has the power to remind your children that Jesus is amazing—and that they, too, can follow Jesus. Use this lesson to share Jesus' life and message with kids, and you'll build a sense of wonder in them that'll inspire them to follow Jesus.

DEPARTURE PRAYER (up to 5 minutes)

Use this on-the-go prayer to get kids on their feet and focused on the wonder of following Jesus.

TOUR GUIDE TIP

If you have a large group, have every other child in line take one giant step forward before you begin praying. This will help kids respect each other's personal space and not get distracted during the prayer.

Have kids line up at one end of the room, while you stand at the opposite wall. Make sure they have a clear path to walk to you.

Say: **I'll say a prayer to begin. I want you to listen closely as I talk to God. Whenever you hear me say the word "follow," take a step toward me.**

Pray: **Dear God,**

There are many people we can choose to *follow*.

When we turn on the TV, we see superheroes and cool characters, each showing us a model to *follow*.

We watch sports and see athletes that we might imitate.

But we know that some are good examples and some are bad examples to *follow*.

We have friends we want to be like.

Help us to *follow* the ones who live like Jesus does.

We listen to music.

Some of the words to the songs help us *follow* Jesus—and some don't. Help us make good choices.

We watch movies. Help us choose ones that help us see what it's like to *follow* you.

Deep down, we want to *follow* you, Jesus,

Because everything you say is true, and everything you do is good.

We want to *follow* you because you know how to help us be good friends with God.

So God, please help us learn to *follow* Jesus even more than we do right now.

In Jesus' name we pray, amen.

1st STOP DISCOVERY

(up to 20 minutes)

Choose-Your-Own Cookie

Use this yummy activity to discuss the benefits of following Jesus.

Show kids the "No-Bake Cookie Recipe" and say: **You all get to make today's snack. Here's a recipe for some yummy cookies. And you have a choice. As a group, you need to vote and decide whether you'll follow this recipe to make the cookies the right way, or come up with your own way to make the cookies. Either way, the end result will be yours to eat.**

Whatever you choose, you'll work as a group. If you choose to follow the recipe, one person will read the first instruction out loud and then follow it. When that person is done, pass the recipe to someone else. You'll keep passing the recipe until everyone gets at least one turn to do something—except step 2, washing up. Everyone does that! I'll help when the instructions tell you to heat up the ingredients. Otherwise, I won't offer much advice unless you ask for it. Let kids look at the recipe and decide what to do. It's very likely they'll choose to follow the recipe.

Once kids have decided what to do, give one child the recipe and have that child read step one. Supervise until kids successfully make the cookies. The cookies will need several minutes to cool. If you have room in your church's refrigerator, you can speed up the process by setting the cookies inside until you're ready to eat them.

When the kids have finished making cookies, return to your room and gather kids around you.

Ask: • **Explain why you chose to follow the recipe—or not.**

• **Describe how the cookies turned out based on the path you chose to follow.**

• **How was this experience like or unlike what happens when we follow someone's example?**

• **How do you choose what kinds of people to follow in real life?**

Say: **You had a choice when you made cookies. You could follow my instructions on how to make the cookies, or you could make them your own way. You could've even chosen to make something other than cookies with the ingredients—maybe something goofy like a statue.**

Historians tell us that in the Ancient Middle East, people made sweet candies with nuts, dried fruits, seeds, and natural sweeteners. But our modern "no-bake" cookies didn't become popular in the United States until the Great Depression when grocery money was scarce and there was renewed emphasis on not wasting anything. No-bake cookies don't require eggs or flour, which made them an excellent choice for a cheap snack.

Items to Pack:

several pictures of pop stars, famous athletes, and national leaders; package of markers for each group; 10 notebook-sized pieces of poster board; large pieces of poster board; glue

TOUR GUIDE TIP

If you need help finding celebrities that kids will recognize, visit the website nick.com/kids-choice-awards/. You'll find a list of actors, musicians, and athletes kids recognize. Look for good role models and not-so-good ones. And bookmark this website. It's an excellent resource to help you keep current with kid culture.

Your world is filled with people you can choose to follow or not follow. Sometimes when we follow someone, things turn out well. But if we follow the wrong person, we can end up in messy situations.

Ask: • **Tell about a time you followed someone only to find out that was a mistake.**

• **Who are good people you've chosen to follow?**

• **What makes those people good leaders?**

Say: **Today we're going to learn about why some people realized they wanted to follow Jesus. We'll discover what they thought was amazing about Jesus and we'll see why ● we want to follow Jesus, too.**

And have no fear! We'll go back for those cookies in a little bit!

STORY EXCURSION

(up to 10 minutes)
What to Follow?

Get your kids voting with their feet and discovering what kind of people they're likely to follow.

Beforehand, search through magazines and the Internet to find pictures of pop stars, famous athletes, and recognizable national leaders such as the president. Cut out 10 or so pictures and use the glue to mount them to notebook-sized pieces of poster board.

Have kids form a line in the center of the room facing you.

Say: **I'm going to show you a picture of a famous person. If this is someone you'd follow, go and stand on the left side of the room. If this is someone you wouldn't follow, then stand on the right side of the room. If you're undecided, stand somewhere in the middle of the room.**

Hold up one of the pictures so kids can see it, and give them time to "vote" by moving to a different place in the room. Between each round, have kids return to the middle line before you hold up another picture and ask them to vote again.

Have kids vote on all the pictures.

Gather kids and ask: • **Explain what helps you decide whether a person is worth following or not.**

• **What were you thinking when some of your friends made different choices than you?**

• **Describe whether you were tempted to change your mind and follow along with your friends' choices.**

Have children form groups of three or four. Give each group a set of markers and a large piece of poster board.

Say: **Work with your group to create an imaginary leader who you all agree would be worth following. You could create a teacher, a musician, an actor, or a politician—it's your choice.**

Work together to draw a picture of the person, and then write a list of things about that person that makes him or her a good leader.

Give the children several minutes to work together to create their super leader. When they're done, have them return to the large group and take turns presenting their leader to the entire group.

Ask: • **Explain whether it was easy or difficult to agree on what would make a great leader.**

• **How would you convince other people that your leader was someone they should follow?**

Say: **In today's Bible passage, people heard about Jesus and decided they wanted to follow him. If we knew what they did about Jesus, we'd probably shout** **we want to follow Jesus, too!**

Ask: • **When someone says, "I'm a fan of" a music star or celebrity, what does that mean?**

• **How is being a fan of someone different from following Jesus?**

Say: **When people say they're fans or they "follow" a popular singer, they likely download the singer's music, memorize words to the songs, and maybe even go to a concert or buy a T-shirt.**

A person who follows a football team might buy that team's jersey and watch all the games. If that fan is really lucky, he or she might get to go to the stadium to watch a real game.

Following Jesus is a lot different from being a fan. Let's play a game to learn more about what following Jesus is like.

Find a partner and stand in front of that person. Pause.

Choose one person to be the Leader and other person to be the Reflection. Pause.

If you're the Leader, it's your job to slowly make a motion. You might wave your hand or pat your head. If you're the Reflection, it's your job to mirror the Leader's every movement as closely as possible.

Have Leaders begin to make their motions for the Reflections to follow. After one minute, have kids switch roles, and then gather kids around you.

Ask: • **Explain what it was like to mimic your partner's every move.**

Items to Pack:

Bible

• **In what way is this game like following Jesus?**

• **How is it different?**

• **We don't have Jesus standing in front of us to imitate. So how do we know what it means to follow him?**

Say: **The Bible tells us what Jesus was like, what he taught, what he did, and how he treated people. Imitating or following Jesus isn't like trying to copy the exact things he did. None of us can make water from wine or walk on water. Following Jesus means trying to make his attitudes and commandments our own.**

Ask: • **What attitudes toward people do you see Jesus demonstrate in the Bible?**

• **What kinds of commandments did he give his followers?**

Say: **Following Jesus means we admit that he knows best and that we try to love God and other people the way he does.** ◓ **We want to follow Jesus, because he's God's Son and he knows the way to live that will make us the happiest. He wants us to join him in God's kingdom**

**ADVENTURES
IN
GROWING**

(up to 10 minutes)

A King Worth Waiting For

This interactive story shows children just how magnetic Jesus was to the people around him.

Open your Bible to Matthew 4:23-25 and say: **Let's turn to Matthew's Gospel and discover this Jesus that people wanted to follow. I'm going to need your help to tell what happened.**

Jesus lived in Israel. The Israelites were God's special people. A long time ago, God promised to be their leader if they'd follow him. So whenever I say "Israel," you say, "We are your people, God."

Let's try that. *Israel.*

If I say "Jesus," I want you to say, "God's Son."

Ready? *Jesus.*

If I say "King," make a crown by touching your thumbs together and your pointer fingers together. Place the crown on your head and say, "Hail to the chief."

Try that. *King.*

Finally, any time I mention any kind of sickness, disability, or people not feeling well, give yourself a hug and moan as if you didn't feel good.

Let's try it. *Chicken pox.*

Excellent!

Quickly review each of the key phrases to ensure children know how to respond.

Say: **Let's tell what happened together:**

A long time ago, God made a special agreement with a group of people known as *Israel*.

God would be their good *king*,

and *Israel's* job was to follow God's good rules.

God wanted *Israel* to be the people who'd introduce everyone to God, their good *king*.

But *Israel* stopped listening to God.

They didn't treat God like their *king* anymore.

They disobeyed his rules and were mean to each other.

God did everything he could to warn *Israel*, but they didn't listen. This made God sad.

Finally, he decided to let another *king* be *Israel's* leader if they didn't want to listen to him.

That's exactly what happened.

Bad *kings* warred against *Israel* and made them live in a faraway country.

And *Israel* became sad.

God wanted to give his people hope, so he sent *Israel* a prophet who told them that someday a special person would come who'd restore God's kingdom.

They'd know they could trust this person because he would make their *deaf people* hear, and their *blind people* see. He would heal all sorts of people.

After many years, the bad *king* let *Israel* return to their home.

But another bad *king* from Rome conquered *Israel* and was very hard on the people.

God's people were sad and remembered the days when God was their good *king*.

Some of them waited and prayed for the day when God's special person would come.

Finally, it happened. There were rumors that there was a man named *Jesus* who was healing people.

He healed people who had *seizures*,

FUN FACT God's people were definitely waiting for a Messiah. History tells us that Jesus wasn't the only person who claimed to be the "appointed one" who'd liberate Israel. Even one of Herod's former slaves, Simon of Peraea, claimed to be the Messiah. And Athronges was a shepherd who became a rebel and also claimed to be the Messiah. But only Jesus performed miracles and preached with power.

Items to Pack:

construction paper, several pairs of scissors, markers or crayons, Travel Journals

And *Jesus* healed people who *couldn't use their legs*,

And *Jesus* healed people who were *bothered by demons*.

He even healed people who *couldn't see* and people who *couldn't hear.*

People got excited and brought their *sick friends* to meet *Jesus*, and he healed them, too.

Wherever *Jesus* went, he taught in their church buildings and told people the good news: The time had come for God to be their good *king* again.

The people were so excited they followed *Jesus* wherever he went—to the country, to the cities, and all over *Israel.*

Ask: • **What do you think God's people learned about choosing who to follow?**

• **Why do you think so many people came to hear Jesus?**

Say: **The people were very excited and curious about who Jesus might be. They heard Jesus preach about God being king again, and they saw Jesus heal their sick friends and family members. And they wanted to follow Jesus.**

Ask: • **What about Jesus makes *us* want to follow him, too?**

Say: **Jesus is our good king. We know that he's loving and he takes care of people. 🌀 We want to follow Jesus.**

SOUVENIRS

(up to 10 minutes)

Follow the Leader

Use this simple craft activity to get kids brainstorming more reasons why they want to follow Jesus.

Say: **We saw in our Bible passage that people definitely wanted to follow Jesus and learn more about him. Jesus got their attention with his teaching and by sharing love and healing with those who were ill.**

But there are more reasons 🌀 we want to follow Jesus. That Bible passage we looked at was from the beginning of Jesus' work on earth. Looking at all that's written about Jesus in the Bible, we know even more about what he's like than the people in the passage did. So let's brainstorm!

Ask: • **What other amazing things does the Bible tell us Jesus did?**

- Explain what you know about how Jesus treats people.
- Tell why you think Jesus is worth following.

Say: **Fishermen quit their lifelong jobs to follow Jesus wherever he went. Crowds of people from all over Israel followed Jesus to hear him talk and have him heal their sick friends. So let's make a foot shape to remind us of all the walking that people did to follow Jesus.**

Distribute construction paper, scissors, and markers or crayons. Have kids place one of their feet on the construction paper and trace around it with a marker. Instruct them to cut their foot shapes out with the scissors.

Say: **There are so many reasons to want to follow Jesus. But what are yours? Write or draw your favorite things about Jesus on your paper foot.**

Give kids time to work. When they're finished, have them form groups of three and share what they wrote or drew.

Say: **It's easy to want to follow Jesus. The Bible is filled with examples of his power and his love. And we know he died on the cross and came back to life so we could have eternal life with God. Jesus wants to be our friend. He's always with us and we can talk to him anytime. So on the count of three, shout out** **"We want to follow Jesus!"**

Ready?

1...2...3... Pause.

Give kids their Travel Journals and have them place their foot shape inside. If you have new kids, give them a folder and have them write their name on it. Then collect the Travel Journals, and put them away till next week.

HOME AGAIN PRAYER _(up to 5 minutes)_

Say: **I bet our cookies are ready.** Lead kids back to the kitchen or arrange in advance for a ministry volunteer to bring the cookies to you after they've cooled and hardened.

Distribute napkins and a cookie to each child. Tell kids not to eat their snack just yet.

Say: **We learned earlier that some leaders are worth following and some aren't. Sometimes we follow people who make bad choices and we end up making the same mistakes they do. Other times we follow people who do their best to be good leaders, but it doesn't work out. But Jesus is our perfect leader.**

Items to Pack:
"no-bake" cookies made earlier, napkins, plastic sandwich bags (optional)

Let's do this: I'll lead you in a prayer. I'll say a line and you'll repeat it. After each line, you can take a bite out of your cookie to remind you how sweet it is to follow Jesus.

Here we go...

Pray: **Dear God, there are a lot of people to follow** (pause).

Some leaders are good and some aren't (pause).

But Jesus is perfect (pause).

He's loving (pause).

He knows what's best for our lives (pause).

Because he's your Son. He's God (pause).

We want to follow Jesus in everything we do (pause).

In Jesus' name, amen.

Distribute the rest of the cookies and let kids enjoy their hard work. If you have a lot of extra cookies, send them home with the children in plastic sandwich bags.

No-Bake Cookie Recipe

INGREDIENTS You'll Need

- ☐ Sugar
- ☐ Butter
- ☐ Milk
- ☐ Unsweetened cocoa powder
- ☐ Vanilla extract
- ☐ Uncooked quick oats
- ☐ Chocolate chips

KITCHEN SUPPLIES You'll Need

- ☐ A glass mixing bowl or medium-sized metal pot
- ☐ A wooden spoon
- ☐ Wax paper
- ☐ Measuring cups and spoons
- ☐ Cookie sheets
- ☐ Microwave oven or a stove top
- ☐ Spoons

TIME You'll Need

- ☐ About 10 to 15 minutes to mix the ingredients and shape the cookies.
- ☐ About 20 minutes for the cookies to harden.

Follow these steps to make some amazingly yummy cookies!

1. Ask your leader to take your group on a walk to the kitchen. Once you get there, ask your leader to decide whether you'll use the stove or the microwave.

2. Scrub in! Wash your hands well with soap before making the cookies. You don't want to spread germs now, do you?

3. Measure 2 cups of sugar. If you're using a microwave oven, dump the sugar into a glass mixing bowl. If you are using a stove, dump it into a pot.

4. Measure a cup of butter. Add that to the sugar.

5. Carefully pour ½ cup of milk into a measuring cup and add that to the butter and sugar.

6. Next, add 4 tablespoons of cocoa to the mixture, and mix well.

7. This is where you're going to need your leader's help to be safe. You're either going to heat the ingredients on the stove until they boil or use a microwave oven. Boil the ingredients for one full minute. If you're using a stove, lower the heat to warm. If you're using a microwave oven, you'll have to hurry through steps eight through eleven to keep the mixture from getting too hard.

8. Smells good, doesn't it? Have someone measure 1 teaspoon of vanilla extract and add it to the warm mixture.

9. Add 1 cup of quick oats to the mix. Got it? Now do it again. And do it again. That's 3 cups total of oats.

10. You'll need a very trustworthy person who won't eat too many chocolate chips. This amazing person must measure ¾ of a cup of chips and add them to the mix.

11. Mix all the ingredients together.

12. Have several people use spoons to make small cookie balls and set them on wax paper-covered cookie sheets to cool.

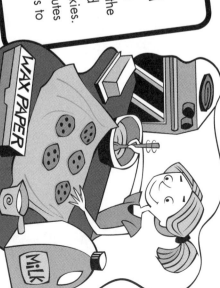

The Sermon on the Mount

Pathway Point: 🔷 Following Jesus' teaching changes our hearts for good.

In-Focus Verse: "One day as he saw the crowds gathering, Jesus went up on the mountainside and sat down. His disciples gathered around him, and he began to teach them" (Matthew 5:1-2).

Travel Itinerary

These verses lead into a teaching by Jesus that's considered by most biblical scholars to be the greatest sermon of all time—the Sermon on the Mount.

As more and more people flocked to hear Jesus speak, the group grew into a great crowd. The fact that so many people were drawn to Jesus illustrates their longing for direction, their need for something more in life. Jesus recognized their needs and spoke to their hearts.

He went up the side of a mountain, stopped, and sat down. A mountain was the perfect place for public speaking, because everyone could see and hear the person addressing the crowd. And it was common in this era for Jewish teachers to sit as they taught.

It's interesting to note that the Sermon on the Mount focuses on internal changes. It focuses on what's inside our hearts—and how we demonstrate these character qualities as followers of Jesus. Jesus' revolutionary teaching was this: Our actions alone aren't enough to save us (directly opposed to what the religious leaders of the time were focused on). It's what's inside our hearts that matters to God. And it's those internal changes that cause us to act in certain ways and not in others.

As you're experiencing this lesson with kids, remember that we all can act more kindly, more friendly, and more like others want us to. But true change comes from within, when we take Jesus' words to heart and let his love shine through us.

Items to Pack:

stick-on nametags, pens

DEPARTURE PRAYER

(up to 5 minutes)

Kids have fun exploring the idea of having a different name and consider what kinds of things might alter their lives.

Say: **Have you ever wished you could have a different name? Like maybe the name of someone famous? Or a silly name like "Cheese Pizza"? Or maybe you'd want to have a name that's easier to spell than yours. If you could change your name, what would you change it to?**

For me, I'd change my name to...

Briefly share what you would change your name to if you had the opportunity. Feel free to make it a funny name so kids see they can have fun with this experience.

After offering your new name, say: **Okay, now it's your turn. Tell what you'd change your name to if you had the chance.**

Let each child tell what he or she would choose for a different name.

Then give each child a nametag and a pen.

Say: **Just for today, let's change our names. Write the new name you'd choose on this nametag and put it on. For our time today, we'll call each other by these new names. So whenever you're talking to other kids today, use only the name on their nametag.**

Allow time for everyone to make a new nametag and put it on. Don't forget to wear a new nametag yourself. Begin calling kids by their new names right away, and try to use the names throughout the entire lesson.

Ask: • **How could having a different name change the way people treat you?**

• **Explain whether you think having a different name would change who you are.**

Say: **Thanks for sharing your thoughts. Today we're going to talk a lot about changes. But not just changes in our names. We'll also be discovering what can change within our hearts. Let's talk to God about this.**

Pray: **Dear God, you know each of us here by name. You know the name our parents gave us, and you know the new names we've just given ourselves.**

You also know what things need to change in our hearts and in our lives. Help us learn today what it means to have a changed heart,

and how following Jesus' teaching changes our hearts for good. In Jesus' name, amen.

Quick Change
(up to 10 minutes)

Kids make small changes in their appearance and observe what others have changed—all to discover that real change isn't on the outside, but in our hearts.

Say: **We've changed our names, and that's going to make our time together a little more fun—and a little more challenging as we try to remember one another's changed names. But what else can we change? We can change how we look.**

I'll go first.

Have all the kids turn their backs to you for a moment. While their backs are turned, change one small thing about your appearance. For example, you might remove a clip from your hair, undo a button on your jacket, untie your shoe, or something else that's quick and easy.

When you're ready, have kids turn back to face you.

Ask: • **Describe what's different or changed about me.**

Allow kids time to look for what you might've changed and call out their ideas. When someone says the correct thing, congratulate that child on his or her observant eyes.

Say: **Now let's all try it.**

Have each child find a partner, and have the pairs stand facing each other. If you have an odd number of children, partner with one of the kids yourself.

Say: **Take a really good look at your partner so you'll know what's changed.**

Give kids a minute, and then have them turn so they're standing back to back and can't see what the other person's doing. When kids are ready, explain that they'll all change one small thing about their appearance. Offer a few suggestions on simple things kids can change, such as pulling up or pushing down socks, taking off glasses, buttoning a sweater, and so on.

Wait a moment while everyone gets ready, and then have kids turn to face each other.

Ask: • **What about your partner changed? Tell your partner what you see that's different.**

After everyone has figured out the changes their partners made, have kids find new partners and play again.

Several people's names changed in the Bible. For example, Abram changed to Abraham, Sarai to Sarah, Jacob to Israel, and Saul to Paul. These name changes reflected an important change that God had in store for these people.

Items to Pack:

Then gather everyone together and ask:

• **Describe how good you were at changing things about your appearance.**

• **What did you do to change your looks?**

• **Describe how observant you were when it came to noticing what was different about your partner.**

• **Tell whether you noticed the changes immediately or if it took you a little time to notice what was different.**

Say: **Thanks for practicing your skills at observation—and for being willing to make a few changes in how you look. If we pay close attention, we can get pretty good at seeing how people change on the outside.**

Ask: • **But what about the inside? For example, if I change my attitude from happy to sad, how would you be able to tell?**

Let kids share ideas on how an internal change might be noticed, such as a change in your facial expression or a change in your actions.

• **What if I changed from being a mean person to being a kind person? How might you be able to tell?**

Say: **People can usually figure out the changes we've made inside our hearts by our actions. But how do we change what's inside our hearts? Today we're discovering that ⏱ following Jesus' teaching changes our hearts for good. Let's keep exploring that idea with another activity.**

Items to Pack:

Bible, large sheets of poster board and markers or a whiteboard and markers

---

STORY EXCURSION

(up to 15 minutes)

Text Messages

Kids play an updated version of the old game Telephone as they discuss what it means to have a changed heart.

Say: **There's a game called Telephone that a lot of your parents probably played when they were younger. In this game the first person in a line would whisper something into the next person's ear, and then people repeated the message down the line to see whether the message would be the same at the end of the line.**

Let's try it!

Have kids line up side by side.

Whisper a silly sentence that'll be a challenge to repeat into one child's ear. For example, "I ate a sauerkraut burger for brunch, then washed my car with a giant mug of root beer." Don't repeat the phrase—just have the child repeat it to the best of his or her ability into the ear of the next child.

Continue down the line, and have the last child in line say aloud what he or she heard to the entire group.

Say: **These days we don't use telephones for talking as much—the majority of us text instead of talk on the phone. So let's change this game a little to be more like texting.**

Write one of the following sentences on the poster board or whiteboard in large letters. You can also use a sentence you create yourself—just be sure that the words you choose can't be easily changed into offensive words.

- We rushed to the store to buy video games that were on sale.
- Please feed the dog before you ride the bus to school.
- Mom said I can have three candies after I eat my carrots.

Say: **Have you ever sent a text message and spelled a word wrong? Or perhaps the phone you were using tried to guess what you were going to type and autocorrected your word to something that wasn't what you meant to say.**

These little changes can make the message different from what we meant to say. Let's try that with this sentence I've written here. What if we changed just one letter in one word? How could that change the meaning of the sentence?

Let kids play around with this and make different suggestions. You can start by changing just one letter in a word or two—and then make more changes a little at a time. If you're using a whiteboard, you can easily replace a letter here and there and kids can see the new message. If you're using a poster board, you can still write the new word in above the old one.

These changes might lead to sentences such as...

- We gushed to the shore to buy video names that were on bale.
- Please seed the hog before you hide the pus to school.
- Mop said I can rake three sandies after I ear my parrots.

Have fun laughing together about the new silly sentences you've created by making small changes.

Ask: • **What do you think was the funniest change we made—and why?**

• **How did such a tiny change—just making one or two letters different—make such a big difference?**

• **Can you think of other things that are changed in a big way with just a tiny change?**

Journey 3: The Sermon on the Mount

An example of this you could share with kids might be a change of direction. If a car is driving in a straight line and the driver moves the steering wheel just a teensy, tiny bit, at first it won't make much of a difference, but within a minute the driver will be in a different lane, and then driving off the road! A super tiny change in direction can lead to a huge change in what happens.

Say: **Little tiny changes can make a great big difference, can't they? This is like the changes that happen in our hearts when we follow Jesus.**

Open your Bible to Matthew 5:1-2.

Say: **The Bible tells us about one time Jesus taught a great big crowd. We're going to be learning more about the important things he said in that talk to the people in the next few weeks. Today let's read Matthew 5:1-2 and see how Jesus' talk started.**

"One day as he saw the crowds gathering, Jesus went up on the mountainside and sat down. His disciples gathered around him, and he began to teach them."

In Bible times they didn't have microphones so everyone was able to hear a speaker. So going outside and sitting on the side of a mountain was a great way to communicate. Everyone could see Jesus sitting a bit higher on the mountain, and they could hear his voice. He sat down, his followers gathered around, and Jesus started teaching them.

The people really wanted to hear what Jesus said. They knew he had something important for them to hear. But if they just listened to the words he said, but didn't *do* anything...what do you think would happen?

Allow kids to think about this and discuss their thoughts.

Say: **I'm sure we can all think of a time when someone, maybe a parent, told us to do something, and even though we heard their words we didn't follow what they said. I can think of a time...**

Tell about a time from your life when you didn't follow someone's good guidance and what happened as a result. Keep your example appropriate to the ages of the kids in your group. For example, you might tell about a time a coach told you what to do during a game and you ignored that and then lost the game—or a story along those lines.

Say: **Hearing someone and ignoring that person doesn't change our hearts. But when we really listen and ● follow Jesus' teaching, it changes our hearts for good.**

ADVENTURES IN GROWING

(up to 10 minutes)

Filled-Heart Sandwiches

You'll all make a snack together, changing the shape of the bread and filling it with good things.

Have kids wash their hands or use hand sanitizer to clean up before you begin this snack.

Say: **It's time for a snack—and this is one that'll keep us talking about how following Jesus' teaching changes our hearts for good.**

Demonstrate how to take one slice of bread and use a heart-shaped cookie cutter to make a heart-shaped piece of bread.

Then have kids work together so that each gets a paper plate with two slices of bread. Take turns using the heart-shaped cookie cutters so each child ends up with two heart-shaped pieces of bread.

Show kids the different toppings. Let each child choose a topping or two to spread on one of the heart shapes, then have kids place the other heart on top to create a simple sandwich. Have kids wait to eat until everyone's finished. Those who finish first can help kids who are still working.

Ask kids to return to their seats with their plates and sandwiches. Let a child who's willing thank God for the snack.

Ask: • **Looking at everyone's sandwiches around you, explain whether you can tell what's inside those hearts.**

Say: **We changed the shape of our bread into hearts—and put something good inside each heart. Some of the hearts have the fillings oozing out—so it's easy to tell what's inside. Others might have a topping that's harder to see from the outside. We'd have to open up the sandwich to see what's in those hearts.**

Let everyone begin eating as you continue.

Ask: • **How do you think others can tell what's inside our hearts?**

• **In what ways do our actions reveal what's in our hearts?**

Say: **It's true that our actions tell people more about our hearts than anything else. Our actions can let others know that we're Jesus' followers.**

After kids finish their snacks, invite them to help you clean up the area, throwing away plates and putting away supplies. Thank everyone for helping.

TOUR GUIDE TIP

Use toppings kids might enjoy. Cream cheese, leftover frosting, jam, dip, chocolate spread—even if you think it's odd, kids might want to give it a try. You don't need enough of each topping for every child—just a variety of toppings so kids can create a filling they think is tasty.

TOUR GUIDE TIP

Cut a slice of the bread with the cookie cutters ahead of time to ensure the bread cuts easily. If the bread doesn't cut easily, bring a sharp knife to help trim off the edges around the cookie cutter. Keep the knife safely away from kids so you're the only one with access to it.

TOUR GUIDE TIP

Save the remaining scraps of bread and take them home to make bread pudding, croutons, or bread crumbs. Or if you prefer, you can use them to feed the birds at a local park.

Items to Pack:

1 copy per child of the "All Ears" handout (at the end of this lesson), crayons or markers, scissors (optional), Travel Journals

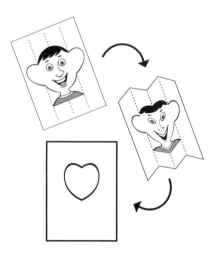

(up to 10 minutes)

All Ears

Kids make a craft that—when folded properly—changes from a picture of a child to a heart.

Say: **Let's make something to help us remember that following Jesus changes our hearts for good—and to give us ideas of actions that show we follow Jesus.**

Give each child a copy of the "All Ears" handout.

Say: **Let's think of actions that would let others know that our hearts have been changed for good because we're following Jesus.**

With kids, brainstorm actions that might show others that they're following Jesus. Keep the direction of ideas realistic, guiding the conversation to ideas that kids actually might do. For example:

• letting a sibling go first when playing a game,

• thanking a parent for making dinner,

• feeding a pet when asked,

• helping wash dishes without being asked, and so on.

After you've talked about a variety of options, have kids each choose two or more ideas that they believe are realistic to do in the coming week.

Say: **When you've decided on a few things that you think you can do this week to let others know you're following Jesus, write or draw those on the ears of your person on the handout.**

Older kids can help younger ones who need help writing.

Say: **Writing the words on our ears is a fun way to remember that we've listened to Jesus' teaching—it's gone into our ears!**

When kids have finished writing, hold up your paper and demonstrate how to fold the page properly:

• Fold the page in half so the narrow ends touch.

• Fold back the two sides along the indicated line.

• When you put the two edges together (as shown in the illustration on this page) the ears of the person form a heart.

Help kids fold their papers properly and have fun showing how the face changes into a heart.

Ask: • **In what ways can this help us remember that 🌐 following Jesus' teaching changes our hearts for good?**

Say: **Thanks for sharing your ideas! It's fun to see this face change from ears that listen—to a heart that shows that we follow Jesus.**

If time permits, let children color the faces. If kids in your group can use scissors, they may cut out the face along the heavier lines.

When kids finish, they can place their "All Ears" souvenir in their Travel Journals. Collect the Travel Journals, and put them away till next week.

HOME AGAIN PRAYER

(up to 5 minutes)

Kids experiment with water by adding salt to make an egg float.

Items to Pack:
2 or 3 washed, raw eggs (check that the shells don't have any cracks); 1 tall clear glass; long spoon; water; salt; tablespoons; paper towels

Say: **Let's try one more thing that makes a change.**

Pour water into the glass so it's more than half full—but leave room to add the egg.

Invite one child to gently place an egg in the water. (You have an extra egg in case there are any accidents.)

The egg will sink to the bottom of the glass. You can add a bit more water at this time if you like, but the glass doesn't need to be completely full.

Say: **This egg sank right to the bottom of the glass. That's kind of like what happens when we have a "sinking" feeling. For example, your best friend says his family is moving away to another state. You get a sinking feeling in your stomach. Or, you thought you did really great on your spelling test, but when you got it back there was a big D on it. Yikes! That causes a sinking feeling. What are other things that might make you have a sinking feeling?**

FUN FACT By adding salt, you're making the water more dense. As you add more salt, the water becomes more and more dense, to the point where the egg will float.

Let kids offer their own "sinking" feelings.

Say: **Thanks for sharing. You know, one thing that can give us a sinking feeling is when we know what Jesus wants us to do—because we've listened to his teaching—but we don't obey. That can really give us a sinking feeling. Let's talk to God about that right now. Let's tell God we're sorry for the times that we don't obey and get that sinking feeling.**

Pray: **Dear God, thanks for listening to us, and thanks for teaching us and changing our hearts. We want to tell you we're sorry for the times we do things that don't show others we follow you. Those things give us a sinking feeling. Please forgive us for those times. In Jesus' name, amen.**

Ask: • **Explain whether you think there's any way to get this egg to float—to get rid of that sinking feeling.**

Yes, involving kids in this experiment increases the risk that an egg will break. But it's so much more fun and engaging for them if they get to participate rather than just watch you. Invite different children to add and remove the egg, to add and stir the water, and so on. Have paper towels on hand and bring along one or two extra eggs just in case one does break. The more relaxed you are about it, the more fun everyone will have—and the more the content of this lesson will stick. It's likely they will show this activity to their family at home—and will remember the Pathway Point as well!

• **What are your ideas?**

Listen to kids' suggestions. They might suggest cracking the egg or using a hard-boiled egg. Explain that none of these ideas will make the egg float.

Say: **What we need to change is the water. Let's experiment.**

Gently remove the egg from the water and set it aside. Let one child add about three tablespoons of salt into the water, have another child stir it well (the water will be cloudy), and then invite a different child to gently return the egg to the water. It's likely that the egg will still sink—but it's fun to experiment.

If the egg sinks, let kids gently remove it and add another three tablespoons of salt. Invite a different child to stir the water (again, it will stay cloudy) and then return the egg to the water. At this point, it should float. (If not, add another round of salt.) Amazing!

Ask: • **What made the difference so the egg would float?**

• **How is adding salt to the water like adding Jesus' teachings to our hearts and actions to get rid of that sinking feeling?**

Say: **This is a change we can see, just like others will be able to see the change in our lives when we follow Jesus' teaching. You can show this experiment to your family and let them know that** ◕ **because you're following Jesus' teaching, your heart is changed for good.**

Let's thank God for taking away the sinking feeling and changing our hearts for good.

Invite any kids who want to thank God for what he's done in their lives to pray. If no one volunteers, you can pray, thanking God for each of the children and the changes that God is making in their lives as they follow Jesus.

Encourage kids to come back next week ready to tell you how following Jesus has made a change in them.

All Ears

JOURNEY 4

God Blesses Those Who Are Poor

Pathway Point: 🌍 God is with us when we're in need.

In-Focus Verse: "God blesses those who are poor and realize their need for him, for the Kingdom of Heaven is theirs" (Matthew 5:3).

Travel Itinerary

In today's society, being "poor" is usually synonymous with existing "without"—lacking in material things. This isn't a circumstance most seek out; it's a condition we aim to avoid. No one wants to be lacking in any aspect of life—financially, emotionally, or relationally. Yet in Matthew 5:3, Jesus makes the radical statement that those who are poor are, in reality, blessed. He said those who realize their need for God—and realize their utter reliance upon him—will be blessed beyond measure.

It's true—poverty of spirit, mind, heart, or pocketbook can serve as a great equalizer. Being without removes the distractions that can pull us in a different direction than toward God. When we're in need, we can more clearly see our reliance on God. When finances run dry, when friends turn their backs, when loneliness and depression take hold—that's when we can't help but open ourselves to receiving God's grace and power. It's in our times of deepest need that we discover God's faithfulness.

Jesus says our utter dependence on God brings blessings from him. It seems an improbable equation, yet it's true. When our resources and strength run out, we encounter God's boundless—endless—love most clearly. Have a humble opinion of yourself. Accept that we are all poor in spirit, in desperate need of a Savior. Ready yourself to go where God leads you and do what he calls you to do. Forget material possessions. Totally and completely surrender your past, present, and future to God's control. When you become poor, you'll truly be blessed.

Items to Pack:

10 inflated, colored balloons and 1 inflated, white balloon for each small group; timer or stopwatch; permanent markers; upbeat music and music player (optional)

TOUR GUIDE TIP

Before you collect supplies for this activity, ensure that none of your kids have latex allergies. If you do have kids with allergies, consider substituting lightweight foam balls for the balloons.

TOUR GUIDE TIP

Consider playing music while kids attempt to keep the balloons afloat. Have groups start the game when the music begins and stop when you turn off the music.

DEPARTURE PRAYER

(up to 5 minutes)

Through this balloon-toss activity and prayer, children discover they can depend on God to provide for all their needs.

Say: **Today we're talking about needs. We're going to see how God blesses people who realize they need him. Let's take a moment to think about the things we *need* to live—like food and water.**

Have kids form small groups. Challenge groups to think of 10 needs. Allow about three minutes for groups to come up with ideas.

Ask the entire group: • **What do you think the difference is between a need and a want?**

After some discussion, give each small group 10 inflated, colored balloons and a permanent marker.

Say: **We need lots of things to live and be happy every day. With your group, take turns using the marker to write one need on each balloon. When you're finished, your group should have 10 "needs" balloons.**

Give groups time to write the needs on their balloons; then have everyone stand.

Say: **Now let's see if you can toss all these needs balloons up into the air at once—and work together with your group to keep them all up for two minutes. Don't let any fall to the floor. If any of your balloons hit the floor, you can't pick them up. Just focus on keeping the rest up. Let's see how you do—ready, go!**

When time's up, ask groups to toss their balloons to one side of the room and remain together.

Ask: • **What was that challenge like for you?**

• **What kinds of needs were you trying to keep in the air?**

• **Explain how successful you were at keeping all the needs in the air.**

• **How was this like or unlike what happens when we try to handle all these needs rather than relying on God to care for our needs?**

Say: **We have a lot of needs in real life, kind of like our game. Even with a lot of people helping, it was very difficult to keep the needs balloons in the air.**

Ask: • **Explain whether you think we can provide for all our own needs.**

Say: **We can't do things all on our own. We can't provide for all our own needs, even though we often start to think we can. God created us to depend on him. God is the only one who can provide for all our needs. Let's explore this more.**

Give each group a white balloon.

Say: **Because we know God provides for all our needs, let's write his name on the white balloon.** Allow time.

On "go," work together with your group to keep the new balloon up in the air for two minutes. Don't let it touch the floor! Ready, go!

Play for two minutes; then have groups set aside their white balloons.

Ask: • **Describe how playing this time was different from the first time.**

• **Explain whether your group was successful at keeping your focus on the new balloon in the air.**

• **How was this game like what happens when we focus on God for all our needs rather than trying to focus on all our responsibilities and needs?**

Say: **When we rely on God for our needs, it's much easier than thinking we have to take care of everything ourselves. God wants us to put our faith and trust in him to take care of us. The truth is, the more we think we can handle everything ourselves, the less we look for and rely on God. But there's no person who can take care of everything. We need God to help us every day, and  God is with us when we're in need.**

Have kids collect and hold all the balloons they set aside earlier and then form a large circle.

Say: **Let's thank God for taking care of our needs and being here for us. I'll start the prayer, then we'll go around the circle and you can each say, "Thank you for (whatever item is on the balloon you're holding)."**

Pray: **God, thanks for providing exactly what we need. Help us learn to depend on you more. We especially want to thank you for...** (Pause, allowing children to fill in the needs from their balloons.)

Once you've gone around the circle, close by saying: **Thank you God, for helping us learn to rely on you because  you're with us when we're in need.**

Quick Draw Hide-and-Seek

Kids feel a sense of need as they experience the setting of the Scripture passage.

Say: **Jesus and his disciples had gathered on a hillside where he was teaching a huge crowd. He was getting ready to tell the people a very important message about God and how to live for him.**

Read aloud Matthew 5:1-2.

Say: **Now I want you to close your eyes and imagine what this experience was like for Jesus' disciples. What would they have seen? What sounds would they have heard? Would it have been hot and dusty, or would it have been chilly and windy? How might it have smelled? What was the crowd like?**

I want you to remember what you were thinking about just now. Got it?

Have kids open their eyes. Distribute a "Quick Draw" handout to each child.

Say: **As Jesus' disciples gathered around him, he began to teach them. His words carried a very important message—and people recognized it. What Jesus said to people during this talk was important because he told people how to live and give their lives to God. Here's the first thing he said.**

Read aloud Matthew 5:3.

Have kids get back in their groups from the previous activity. Say: **Before we discuss what that verse means, I'd like you to do a "quick draw" picture. Think back to what you imagined earlier about what it might have been like to sit on the hill below Jesus and listen while he talked. Remember what the scene might've looked like, and draw your picture in the space under the verse. Remember to include what the disciples would've seen, heard, felt, and experienced while they were there with Jesus. And remember, this is a "quick draw." That means you don't have much time to draw—so only include the important elements. You'll have five minutes.**

Give each group a bag of crayons to draw their pictures—but don't mention that each bag is missing all shades of blue, green, and brown.

Walk around the room and encourage kids as they begin drawing. You'll hear first questions, then complaints, about the colors that are lacking. Don't interfere in the conversation—soon the entire group will be discussing the colors they need to draw the picture. Don't comment on the color issue as you walk around, and if a child approaches you asking for the missing colors, say: **All the colors you need are in the bag.** After a few minutes, call time.

Ask: • **Describe what it was like to draw your picture.**

• **Explain what was obviously missing for you to be able to draw your picture—and what you did about it.**

• **How was this experience like or unlike what happens when we're lacking something important in real life?**

• **Explain what you think it's like to need something you don't have.**

Say: **Even though you didn't have what you needed to complete your picture, you could still create. It may not have been the picture you originally imagined, but you still made a drawing that was unique and represented Jesus to others. That's like real life. We may not always have everything we need, but we can rely on ⬤ God to be with us when we're in need. He'll help us take what we have and live a life that reflects Jesus to others. We can always depend on God to provide for our needs.**

STORY EXCURSION

(15 minutes)

Soak Up More

Kids realize that being in need helps them soak up more of God's blessings.

Say: **We just experienced what it's like to be in need. You couldn't provide yourself with what you needed for your picture. That's a little like how it feels to be lacking things in real life. Remember what Jesus said in Matthew 5:3: "God blesses those who are poor and realize their need for him, for the Kingdom of Heaven is theirs." When we realize that we're in need, we also realize how much we depend on God. That makes us more able to soak up his love. It's easy to begin thinking that we can take care of our needs all on our own. Many people don't recognize that they need God. They try to fill themselves with lots of material possessions or other things. But they're still empty inside. Let's look at a few important supplies that'll help us make room for God's love in our lives.**

Items to Pack:
For each pair of kids: 1 light-colored, dry sponge cut in half; bowl filled with water; large medicine dropper (inexpensive versions available at drug stores). Also: 1 pitcher of water tinted red with food coloring or unsweetened drink mix

TOUR GUIDE TIP
Practice ahead of time to see how much water a sponge can absorb without leaking. If the sponges are extremely absorbent, you may tell kids to fill their dropper twice for each item listed.

Have kids form pairs. Give each pair a dry sponge piece, a bowl of water, and a medicine dropper. Set a pitcher of red-tinted water nearby.

Say: **We're going to pretend that we're like these sponges. We have choices to make every day—to soak up more of God's love or to fill our lives with things our world considers important.** Have both partners take turns holding the sponge.

Ask: • **Describe what your sponge feels like right now.**

Say: **Right now the sponge is dry, hard, and empty. It's ready to soak up water.**

Now you're going to work with your partner to think of the kinds of things that our world wants us to fill our lives with—things like fancy cars or lots of video games. Each time you name something, one partner will fill the dropper with water and squirt it onto the dry sponge while the other partner holds the sponge. Hold the sponge over the bowl to catch any drips.

Let kids think of ideas for a couple of minutes, then have them switch roles and continue. Listen—and offer ideas—as kids name things that the world considers important. Some examples could include material things, lots of activities and sports, celebrity, importance, power, money, and so on. Tell kids to stop naming things when their sponge is full and overflowing into the bowl. Tell them to not wring out the water, but to continue holding the wet sponge.

Ask: • **How do you know whether your sponge is full?**

• **Tell about some of the things you filled the sponge with.**

• **What happened when you filled the sponge with too many things?**

Say: **When life is full of things the world wants us to care about, it leaves little room for God and the things he wants us to care about. Let's see if we can add a dropper full of God's love to our sponge. I have a special pitcher of red water to represent God's love for us. I'll walk around and let you fill your dropper from my pitcher of God's love. Once you've filled your dropper, squirt it onto your sponge and see what happens.**

Have kids fill their dropper again and release it onto the sponge.

Ask: • **What happened to the water that represented God's love?**

• **Explain whether there was any room left in the sponge for God's love.**

• **How is this like or unlike what happens when we focus on all these other things rather than God's love?**

Say: **It's important to spend time with God and soak up lots of his love. If we try to handle everything ourselves and fill our lives with stuff the world says is important, we don't leave much room for God in our lives.**

Let's try this again. Squeeze your sponge into the bowl so the sponge is almost dry.

Allow time.

Say: **Now hold your sponge over the bowl again. This time we're going to fill up our sponges with God's love.** Walk around with the pitcher of tinted water and say: **As I pour the water onto your sponge, watch it soak up God's love until it overflows.** Walk around and pour the tinted water onto each sponge, ensuring kids hold the sponges over the bowls.

When you've poured the water over all the sponges, ask:

• **Explain which time the sponge soaked up God's love the best and why.**

• **What does this experiment tell you about the difference between filling our lives and letting God fill our lives?**

Say: **When we're "poor" in the eyes of the world, we actually have more room to soak up God's love and presence. When we choose not to fill our lives with stuff that doesn't matter, it's easier for us to be filled to overflowing with God's love.**

ADVENTURES IN GROWING

(15 minutes)

Trail Mix Bar

Kids realize that God is with them when they're in need—providing for them in ways they don't always expect.

Say: **God is with us when we're in need. He provides for us, and we need God more than anything else. As we think about what it means to rely on God when we're in need, we're going to make special trail mix.**

Have kids form groups of four or fewer. Distribute a different ingredient to each group and a resealable bag for each child.

Ask: • **Describe what your favorite ingredient in trail mix tastes like.**

• **Look at the ingredient I just gave your group. Explain whether you have everything you need to make a bag of trail mix.**

• **What kinds of ingredients are missing?**

TOUR GUIDE TIP

This lesson requires a variety of ingredients. You can gather ingredients for the trail mix bar in advance or simply ask parents to bring a specific ingredient for this lesson. Suggested ingredients include: cereals (include some gluten-free varieties), different types of dried fruit, yogurt raisins, chocolate and white chocolate chips, M&M's candies, marshmallows, pretzels.

• **Explain whether you think I'll give you everything you want to make your trail mix.**

• **Discuss with your group whether everything you *want* is the same as everything you *need*.** Allow time.

Say: **God is always with us, especially when we're in need. Sometimes he gives us what we want; sometimes he gives us what we need. They're not always the same thing.**

Show kids the other ingredients you've set aside.

Ask: • **What do you see that you'd like to add to your trail mix?**

Say: **In a minute, you'll be able to add these ingredients in your trail mix.**

Another way God provides for us is through others.

Ask: • **Tell about a time someone else helped you or provided for you.**

• **Look at the other groups' ingredients. What ingredients do you see that you'd like to add to your trail mix?**

• **Why do you think God has other people help us and provide for us when we're in need?**

Let each group hold up their ingredient and tell the larger group what they have.

Say: **We'll share our ingredients with other groups in just a minute.**

Ask: • **Explain what other ingredients you'd like that we don't have.** Pause for discussion.

Say: **Sometimes God knows that we don't *need* everything we *want*. When we depend on God to provide for us, we admit that he knows what's best for us. Will all our trail mix combinations be the same? No! We all need different things. Through it all, ⬤ God is with us when we're in need, giving us exactly what we need, when we need it. Let's pray and thank God for this delicious snack and his faithfulness.**

Pray: **Dear God, thank you for providing for our needs. Thank you for filling us with your love and helping us learn to rely on you rather than trying to handle everything ourselves. Thank you for providing us with this snack today. In Jesus' name, amen.**

Say: **Let's gather all our ingredients and take turns filling our bags with just the right combination of ingredients.**

Set up the ingredients and serving utensils where children can move through the line choosing their favorite ingredients and adding them to their bags. Let kids enjoy their snacks while they complete their Travel Journals.

SOUVENIRS

(10 minutes)

Travel Journals

Kids create cards for their Travel Journals that remind them God is the answer to all their needs.

Items to Pack:
Bibles; index cards with two Scripture references written on one side: Philippians 4:19 and 2 Corinthians 9:8; pens or pencils; red markers, Travel Journals

Say: **We've heard Jesus say it's good for us to be "needy" and "poor." We've learned that ⬤ God is with us, providing for us when we're in need. We also discovered that God doesn't always give us what we want because sometimes what we want is different from what we need—and he knows best.**

I'll give each of you an index card. Work with a partner to create a list of things you need—not things you want—on the blank side. Distribute Bibles, pens or pencils, and the Travel Journals. Ask for a few examples of needs versus wants, and allow time.

Say: **Let's see what the verses on the back of the card tell us about how God provides for our needs.** Have kids work together to find and read the passages. Allow time; then gather kids' attention.

Ask: • **Explain whether you think these verses back up what Jesus said.**

• **What do you think these verses tell us about God?**

• **Why do you think God provides for our needs?**

• **What's one thing you can rely on God for this week?**

Say: **These verses tell us that God is the answer to our needs.**
⬤ He's always with us, providing for us when we are in need.

Distribute a red marker to each pair of kids.

Say: **God's always there for us. To remind us of this, take the red marker and write "GOD" in large letters over the list of needs you wrote on the card.**

Allow time, and then have kids place their cards in their Travel Journals. Collect the Travel Journals, and put them away till next week.

Items to Pack:

1 copy per child of the "Socks of Love" handout (at the end of this lesson)

TOUR GUIDE TIP

If you have younger kids who struggle with letters, encourage them to think of one thing that they consider a blessing.

TOUR GUIDE TIP

If your group is too large or you're pressed for time, have children circle up and pray in groups.

HOME AGAIN PRAYER

(up to 5 minutes)

Kids thank God for providing for them and learn how God can help them provide for others.

Say: **Remember how we discovered that sometimes God provides what we need through other people? Well, this week God can help you reach out to someone in need. I'll give you a handout that has directions for making some Socks of Love at home. You'll buy a new pair of long socks and a few trial-size hygiene items such as soap, toothbrush, toothpaste, shampoo, or hand sanitizer. You'll roll up one sock, push it inside the other sock, and then stuff all the hygiene items inside. Last, tie the top of the sock closed with some curling ribbon or yarn, and bring your bundle in next week. Then we'll give them to a local shelter to help provide for someone else's needs.**

Distribute the handout to children and encourage them to bring in their Socks of Love next week.

Say: **God wants us to depend on him. Let's thank God for providing for us in amazing ways and for always being with us.**

Think of something God provides for you that starts with the first letter of your first name. So if your name is Anna, think of something that starts with an A.

Give kids time to think and respond.

Say: **Now let's turn those things into a prayer to God. I'll start by naming an item that starts with the first letter of my name. Then you'll each take turns, repeating this sentence and adding your item. Let's pray.**

Pray: **God, thanks for providing me with _____** (name an item that starts with the first letter of your first name).

Let kids take turns repeating the prayer with the same sentence. After the last child has prayed, close the prayer.

Pray: 🌑 **God, you're always with us. You take care of our needs. You're all we need. Thank you! In Jesus' name, amen.**

God blesses those who are poor and realize their need for him, for the Kingdom of Heaven is theirs" — Matthew 5:3.

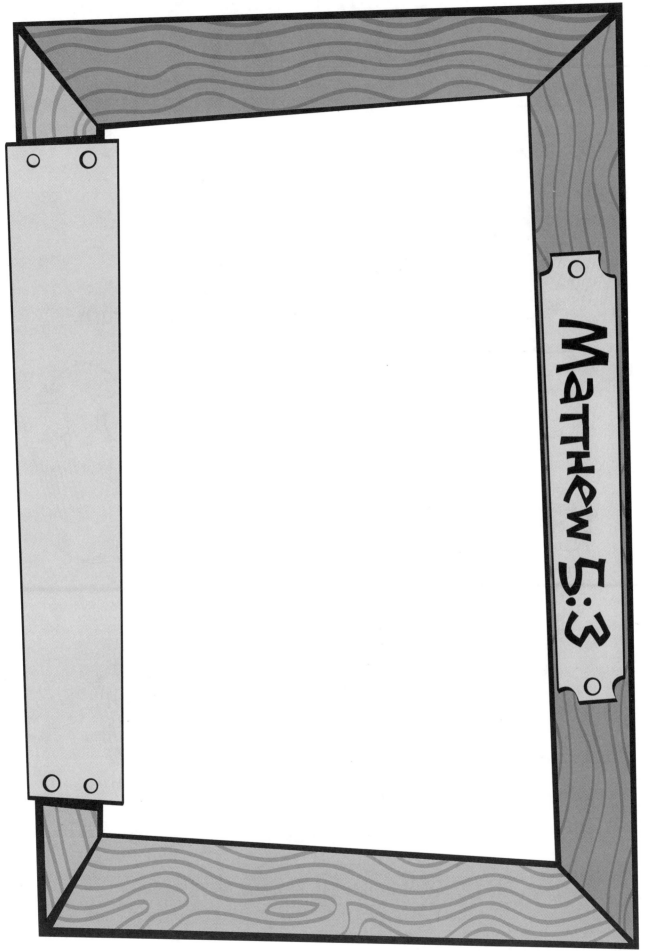

MATTHEW 5:3

Socks of Love

Your child is learning that God is with us when we're in need. The kids also learned that sometimes God provides for us through the generosity of others. This week, your family can reach out to others in our community by making "Socks of Love" and bringing them in next week. Here's what to do:

1 Purchase a new pair of long socks.

2 Purchase trial-size hygiene items such as soap, toothbrush, toothpaste, shampoo, hand sanitizer, and so on.

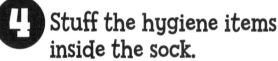

3 Roll up one sock and stuff it inside the other. Push it down to the very bottom of the sock.

4 Stuff the hygiene items inside the sock.

5 Tie the top closed with some curling ribbon or yarn.

6 Bring this gift next week so we can deliver the Socks of Love to a local program.

Thank you for providing for others' needs!

God Blesses Those Who Are Sad

JOURNEY 5

Pathway Point: God comforts us when we hurt.

In-Focus Verse: "God blesses those who mourn, for they will be comforted" (Matthew 5:4).

Travel Itinerary

It doesn't usually feel like sadness is a blessing. In fact, it can feel like the exact opposite. However, it's often in our lowest times that we draw closer to God. As we lean on God's promises, we learn more about him and the plans he has for us.

Sadness is an emotion we all feel at some point. The Bible gives multiple accounts of times even Jesus felt loss and sadness. When he heard of his cousin John the Baptist's death, Jesus went to be alone (Matthew 14:13). Upon hearing of his friend Lazarus' death, Jesus was moved not only to tears but also to weeping (John 11:35).

It can be a difficult thing, finding the right words to say in times of sorrow. We want to provide comfort and hope, but it's important not to minimize or discount others' feelings of sadness. When you talk to children about sadness, validate their feelings. Avoid saying things such as "God doesn't want you to be sad," or "God will only give you what you can handle." Children need to know it's okay to feel sad, and they need appropriate outlets for the emotions they feel.

As in your own life, be sensitive to the experiences your children have had, such as divorce or death. Everyone deals with loss and sadness in different ways, and while some children may want to talk openly, others may feel uncomfortable doing so. Guide conversations as needed. Tell about your own experiences. Don't press kids to open up, but invite them to. Sadness is something we all experience in varying degrees—and Jesus got that. He knew all too well that this life is plagued by sadness, and he offered great hope in God through his words.

To keep this lesson from focusing too much on sadness, continue to point children to God's comforting presence through Jesus' words in Matthew 5:4. We may experience sadness in this world, but we have comfort in God's love and care for each of us.

TOUR GUIDE TIP

Children will respond in different ways to the sour candy. Some will act like the candy is too sour, while others may act like it's not sour at all. Use those reactions to spur discussion. Just as we react differently to the sour candy, we respond differently to feelings of sadness. No matter how we respond, God is there to comfort us.

DEPARTURE PRAYER   (up to 5 minutes)

In this prayer, children experience how God can turn a sour experience into something sweet.

Have children sit in a circle.

Say: **Think of a time when you lost something or someone special to you. For me, a time I lost someone or something was...**(briefly tell about a time you lost someone or something special).

Say: **Now it's your turn. Find a partner and tell about when you lost someone or something special.**

Help kids form pairs or trios. Walk around the room, encouraging kids to talk. And be patient; don't press kids if they don't volunteer a response.

After one minute, say: **Okay, switch! Let the next person share.** After another minute, continue.

Say: **Thank you for telling your story. It can be hard talking about loss, but it helps knowing others have felt it, too.**

Ask: • **Describe what it was like for you when you lost something or someone so important.**

• **What did you do during that experience?**

Show kids the candy.

Ask: • **Show me a face you might make when you eat something sour.**

• **Describe what it's like to taste something so sour.**

Say: **Losing someone or something can make us feel really bad inside. In fact, it can feel downright sour—like these super-sour candies.**

This candy can be very sour when you first experience it. However, when you keep it in your mouth long enough, something amazing happens. It turns from sour to sweet. The same thing can happen when we feel sad. When we hurt, it can feel like these sour candies taste. We're learning today that ⬤ God comforts us when we hurt. As we rely on him when we feel so bad inside, he can turn our sadness into something very sweet.

I'm going to give each of you a piece of sour candy. Hold it in your mouth without taking it out. As I pray, I want you to eat the candy and thank God for turning our sour sadness into sweet comfort.

56

Distribute one piece of candy to each child. Remind them to wait to eat it until you begin praying.

Say: **Please bow your heads with me as I pray. You can eat the candy as I start praying.**

Pray: **Dear God, thank you for hearing our prayers. Sometimes life can be sour and make us feel very sad inside. We know that when we're sad or hurting, you're with us. We pray that in those times we'll feel your comfort. Thank you for turning something sour into something sweet. In Jesus' name, amen.**

If you have enough extra candy, let kids eat a few more pieces just for fun. As they eat, tell about a time when God comforted you. How did he comfort you? Did he give you a specific verse or send someone your way with words of encouragement?

1st STOP DISCOVERY

(15 minutes)
Guess the Emotion

In this experience, kids act out and explore different emotions.

Items to Pack:
slips of paper, pens or pencils, bucket or hat to collect slips of paper

Ask kids to sit together in a circle.

Say: **Let's play a guessing game! God created us to have many different emotions. When we feel a different emotion, our bodies can "take over" and act differently. Our faces change, our body language changes. We might even make different sighs or sounds. Each one of you is going to get a chance to act out an emotion without speaking, and the rest of the group will guess what it is.**

First, let's get creative as we think of different emotions. Act out how you'd feel in these different situations—but don't speak.

- **You get an A on your spelling test.**
- **You can't find your homework.**
- **Your sister broke your favorite toy.**
- **Your soccer team won the championship.**
- **Your friend gets the new shoes you've been wanting.**

Distribute slips of paper and pens or pencils.

Say: **On your slip of paper, write or draw an emotion—and be creative. I'll add the emotions "happy" and "sad" first, so don't use those. When you're done, place your paper in the bucket.**

Items to Pack:

Bible, 1 paper plate per child, pens or pencils, construction paper, an assortment of craft supplies such as crayons, markers, scissors, glitter glue, ribbon, chenille wires, and sequins

Write "happy" and "sad" on paper slips and add them to the bucket. Then have children write one emotion on each slip of paper, helping them as needed. Collect the slips of paper in the bucket.

Say: **Now we're going to take turns acting out these different emotions. Everyone will get to act. Some people might get the same emotion to act; that's okay! We might act differently even when we feel the same emotion. If you want to guess the emotion someone's acting out, raise your hand. If you guess correctly, you get to act next. And remember, no speaking when you're acting.**

Choose the child whose birthday is next to go first. Have the child choose a slip of paper from the bucket and act out the emotion for the group. As kids guess which emotion the child is acting, be sure to call on different children. Don't stop the game until each child has had a chance to act.

When each child has had a chance to act, gather everyone's attention back to you.

Say: **Wow—that was a roller coaster of emotions!**

Ask: • **Why do you think God created us to have different emotions?**

• **Describe some emotions you like to feel—and why you like them.**

• **Describe emotions you don't like to feel—and why.**

• **Explain where you think God is when we feel good emotions. when we feel unhappy emotions.**

Say: **Some emotions can be more fun than others, like how we feel when we're playing with a friend. And some emotions aren't so fun, like when we lose someone or something important to us. But we can always remember: ◐ God comforts us when we hurt.**

STORY EXCURSION

(10 minutes)

Nehemiah Feels Sad

Kids react to Nehemiah's emotions while hearing about his experience from the Bible.

Have kids stand. Say: **Show me a sad face. Now show me a happy face. Those are beautiful smiles!**

Distribute one paper plate to each child.

On your paper plate, I want you to draw a sad face on one side and a happy face on the other side.

Give kids a couple of minutes to draw. When they're finished, bring kids' attention back to you.

Say: **We've been learning about different emotions today, especially sadness. Right now I'm going to tell you about a man in the Bible named Nehemiah, who was very, very sad. As I read, listen carefully to how Nehemiah feels. Whenever you think Nehemiah is sad, turn your plate to the sad side. When you think Nehemiah is happy, turn your plate to the happy side.**

Open your Bible to Nehemiah 1.

Say: **Nehemiah was a Jewish man. He and his family were from Jerusalem. Nehemiah lived in King Artaxerxes' palace in Persia. He was a cupbearer—an official whose duty was to serve drinks at the royal table.**

One day, one of Nehemiah's brothers came to visit from Jerusalem. He told Nehemiah that things weren't well in Jerusalem. The wall of Jerusalem had been torn down and the gates destroyed by fire. Show me with your plates how Nehemiah might've felt.

Have kids show you the sad side of their plates.

Ask: • **Explain why you think Nehemiah was sad.**

Say: **Nehemiah was very sad about what had happened. Jerusalem's walls were in ruins. In Bible times, cities had walls to protect the people inside from enemies. Without a wall, the people, including his family, could be attacked or hurt.**

Nehemiah was so sad that he wept. He fasted, cried, and prayed for days. He prayed that God would hear his prayers, and that the king would be kind to him.

Ask: • **What does it mean to you that Nehemiah turned to God for comfort in his sadness?**

• **When have you turned to God for comfort?**

Say: **Let's read what happened when Nehemiah went to the king.**

Read aloud Nehemiah 2:1-8. Prompt kids to hold up their plates to correspond with Nehemiah's feelings as you read.

Ask: • **How do you think the king knew Nehemiah was sad?**

Say: **Let's find out what happened when Nehemiah arrived in Jerusalem.**

Read aloud Nehemiah 2:16-18, continuing to prompt the kids to respond with their paper plates.

FUN FACT A cupbearer was an officer in the royal courts whose job was to serve wine to the king. He sometimes had to taste the wine before serving it to test for poison.

TOUR GUIDE TIP

Natural disasters such as hurricanes, earthquakes, and floods are a common occurrence. The effect they can have on families is devastating. If a disaster has recently occurred, children may want to talk about it. Remind kids of God's comfort, and help them think of ways they can show God's love to people who've been affected.

TOUR GUIDE TIP

Crushed glass is available at craft stores. This prepackaged glass is specially treated so sharp edges are dulled. This is a project for kids age 5 and older with adult supervision; crushed glass presents a choking hazard for younger children.

Items to Pack:

Bible, Christmas ornament you can break, large paper bag, hammer, protective eyewear, work gloves (optional) 1 copy per child of the "Happiness Mosaic" handout (at the end of this lesson) copied onto card stock, glue, crushed glass, Travel Journals

Say: **Nehemiah and the people went on to rebuild the wall of Jerusalem. Even though they faced threats from an enemy, they finished the wall in only 52 days! That must've made Nehemiah very happy!**

Nehemiah was far away from home when he heard the sad news about Jerusalem. In his sadness, Nehemiah prayed to God and God heard his prayers. The king allowed Nehemiah to rebuild the wall because ◐ God comforts us when we hurt.

Unfortunately, many people experience what Nehemiah went through. People lose their homes to fires, tornadoes, floods, hurricanes, earthquakes, and other disasters.

Ask kids if any of them have experienced such a situation, and let them tell about it if they wish.

Say: **King Artaxerxes saw Nehemiah's sadness and offered to help. We can be like the king and help those who've experienced loss, such as people who have lost their homes.**

Ask: • **What are ways we can bring comfort to people who've lost their homes?**

Say: **Let's make cards to give to people who've suffered loss. In our cards, we can write words of comfort and encouragement.**

Ask: • **What kinds of comforting words can we write?**

Briefly allow kids to voice words of comfort.

Say: **Those are great ideas. Let's also remember to tell them that ◐ God comforts us when we hurt.**

Give children time to decorate their cards and write comforting words. When kids finish, collect the cards to send to those in need.

Some kids may want to give their cards to someone they know, which is a great idea. If kids decide to turn in their cards, collect them and give them to people in your congregation or community. If a recent disaster has occurred, contact the Red Cross (redcross.org) to send your cards to those affected.

ADVENTURES IN GROWING

(15 minutes)
Near the Brokenhearted

Children create a mosaic from crushed glass.

Read aloud Psalm 34:18.

Say: **Sometimes when we're sad, it can feel like our hearts are broken or crushed. This verse tells us that God is near us when we feel that way.**

Show kids the Christmas ornament.

Say: **This ornament is so pretty. Ornaments like these remind us of happy times, like Christmas and family.**

Place the ornament inside the paper bag.

Say: **This ornament is like us. It's whole and happy, but sometimes sad things happen, like our parents divorcing or a grandparent dying or a pet getting lost. When sad things happen, it can feel like our whole world is falling apart.**

Tap the ornament gently through the bag with the hammer until it breaks. Take out one piece of the ornament and show kids.

Say: **When we're sad and hurting, we can feel like this ornament is now—crushed and broken. We wonder if we'll ever feel whole again. We wonder if God can ever put the pieces of our heart back together.**

Keep the rest of the broken pieces in the paper bag and dispose of it properly.

Say: **Our ornament is in many little pieces, but we can take those pieces and make something new.**

Give each child a card-stock copy of the "Happiness Mosaic" handout.

Say: **We're going to make mosaics on our papers using crushed glass. This glass was once something whole and beautiful, like a vase or drinking glass. Now it's crushed into many little pieces like our ornament. Let's see how we can take something sad and broken and turn it into something beautiful.**

Explain to kids that they'll glue the glass onto their paper. They can make different designs or pictures of anything that makes them happy, such as a flower, person, or rainbow.

Allow time for children to complete their mosaics. Kids may want to draw pictures with a pencil first, and then glue on the crushed glass. When kids finish, collect the papers and set them aside to dry.

Say: **Today we've learned that** **God comforts us when we hurt. He takes all those broken pieces and makes something new and beautiful. Let's think of ways he can comfort us in a sad situation. I'm going to read different examples, and I want you to come up with a way God might comfort us and turn something sad into something beautiful.**

Read the following list and encourage kids to give ideas of how God comforts us. Give prompts if needed.

FUN FACT

Psalm 34 is an acrostic poem. Each verse begins with a successive letter of the Hebrew alphabet. If you have extra time, consider having kids write their own acrostic poems using the word COMFORT.

TOUR GUIDE TIP

Safety Note: When breaking the ornament, wear protective eyewear. You may also want to wear work gloves. Make sure children are at least 10 feet away from the breaking ornament. When you're finished, dispose of the ornament pieces properly inside the bag you broke it in.

SCENIC ROUTE →

For younger children, or if crushed glass isn't feasible, use ripped construction paper or foam mosaic stickers (available at craft stores).

TOUR GUIDE TIP

For easy cleanup, place newspaper under the mosaic projects. Have children tap excess glass onto the newspaper. Then simply roll up and throw away the newspaper when everyone's done.

- **Your best friend moves to a different state.** (You might stay in touch and be lifelong friends. You might meet new friends in your best friend's absence.)
- **Your grandma is sick and now has to live with you.** (You get to learn more about your grandma than you would have if she'd not moved in.)
- **Your dad has lost his job.** (He finally gets time to pursue a hobby he loves, and maybe that becomes his new job!)
- **Your team lost an important game.** (But you learn key ways your team can work together better, and you win the next game because of what you learned by losing.)

Ask: • **Tell about a time something sad happened to you, but it turned out okay.**

- **In that situation, how did God comfort you?**
- **How did others comfort or encourage you?**
- **What are ways we can comfort others when they feel sad?**

Say: **We all experience loss and sadness. God never promised we wouldn't feel sad. But we can hold on to his promise that**  **God comforts us when we hurt.** Have kids put the mosaics in their Travel Journals.

SOUVENIRS →

(10 minutes)

Coping With Sadness

This experience helps kids discover ways to cope with sadness.

Give each child a copy of the "Cheer Up!" handout.

Say: **It's okay to feel sad sometimes, but we can learn how to handle those feelings so they don't become too overwhelming. That means we need to find a way not to feel sad anymore.**

Ask: • **What helps you feel better when you're sad?**

- **Describe some games or activities that cheer you up.**

Say: **When we're sad, thinking of something funny, like a favorite joke, can really help.**

Tell kids an appropriate joke, if you know one.

Say: **Jokes make us laugh. Find a partner and share a favorite joke.**

Have kids get in pairs or trios. Give them one minute to share jokes. If kids don't know a joke, encourage them to make up a silly knock-knock joke.

Items to Pack:

Bibles, pens or pencils, 1 copy per child of the "Cheer Up!" handout (at the end of this lesson), Travel Journals

SCENIC ROUTE → Laffy Taffy candy has jokes printed on the wrapper. Give each of your kids a piece of Laffy Taffy and let them take turns sharing the jokes.

Say: **Laughing usually makes us feel better, especially when we're only a little sad. But sometimes, we can feel sad for a very long time, such as when we lose someone very close to us. There's no right or wrong length of time to feel sad. But when we're sad for a while, we might need to talk to someone who can help us with our sadness. We can always remember to talk to God, too, because he comforts us when we hurt.**

Ask: • **Tell about a person you can talk to when you're sad.**

Say: **When you're feeling sad, you can talk to a parent, teacher, or maybe a counselor. If you feel sad for a long time, it's a good idea to ask for help. But a lot of times, you can look for ways to feel better by yourself, starting with talking to God and asking him to help you feel better.**

We're going to take the next few minutes to answer the questions on our "Cheer Up!" handout. Then, whenever you're feeling sad, you can pull it out and use it to cheer up!

Let kids complete their handouts and then place them in their Travel Journals. Collect the Travel Journals, and put them away till next week.

HOME AGAIN PRAYER _____ (up to 5 minutes) _____

Place three blocks in a row at the front of the room, each with a sticky note on it. On one note write "G," on the next "O," and on the third "D." Give each child a sticky note and a block.

Say: **Think of something that makes you sad right now that you'd like to talk to God about. Maybe it's a situation you're going through, such as losing a pet or a problem with a friend. Maybe you want to pray for someone you know, such as a friend who's moved away or lost their house. In a minute, I'll play a worship song. While the song plays, think of a request you have for God and write or draw it on your sticky note.**

Start the music and let kids silently write or draw their prayer requests. Walk around the room to help guide requests.

After a couple of minutes, say: **Now stick the note to your block. When you've done that, bring your block up and place it on top of one of the three blocks at the front.**

Help kids build a wall with their blocks.

Items to Pack:
pens or pencils; 1 large block per child, plus 3 additional blocks; sticky notes; soft worship music, a music player

SCENIC
ROUTE
→

If you have space, consider painting a portion of your wall with chalkboard paint to create a more permanent prayer wall. Each week children can write their prayer requests and erase them when they've been answered.

Say: **This wall reminds me of the wall Nehemiah built. God comforted Nehemiah and helped him rebuild the walls of Jerusalem. Our prayer wall is built on God. It reminds us that 🌑 God comforts us when we hurt.**

Say: **Before we close, look at one more thing. Each of your blocks is held up by someone else's. If I take one of those blocks out, the whole wall will tumble. In the same way, we can comfort one another and lift each other in prayer. Each of you, please come up and choose someone else's block.**

Allow time for children to come and take a block other than their own.

Say: **You'll take home someone else's sticky note. Stick the note somewhere where you'll remember to pray for that need—maybe on your mirror, Bible, or locker at school. As you pray for someone else, be comforted knowing that someone else is praying for you, too.**

Let's pray. Stand with your hands at your side and your heads bowed. We're going to pray for each other.

Pause so children can pray.

Pray: **Thank you, God, for hearing us and comforting us. In Jesus' name, amen.**

HAPPINESS MOSAIC

God Heals My Broken Heart

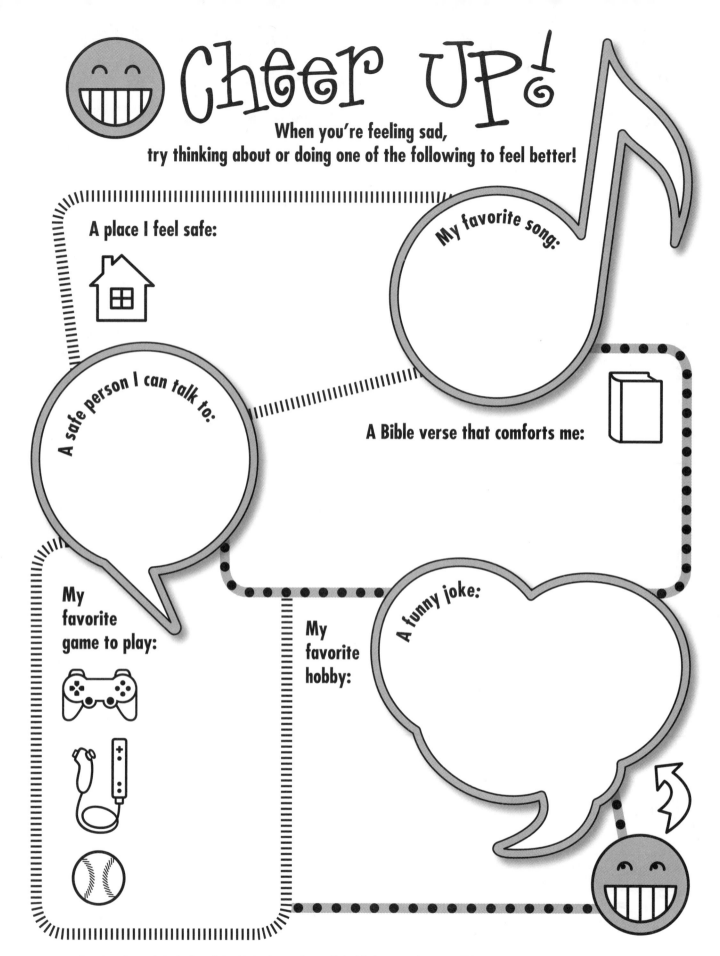

Cheer UP!

When you're feeling sad,
try thinking about or doing one of the following to feel better!

A place I feel safe:

My favorite song:

A safe person I can talk to:

A Bible verse that comforts me:

My favorite game to play:

My favorite hobby:

A funny joke:

God Blesses Those Who Are Gentle and Kind

Pathway Point: ⬤ God will reward us in heaven.

In-Focus Verse: "God blesses those who are humble, for they will inherit the whole earth" (Matthew 5:5).

Travel Itinerary

For many children, all of life seems a competition—for their parents' time and attention, for the best grade in school, for a spot on a sports team. In a world where they're pushed to be the best, humility can seem like a faraway concept. But humility is actually very simple. In fact, it's really no different from the golden rule: Treat others the way you want to be treated.

This lesson focuses on Jesus being our truest example of humility and what it means to put others first. Jesus said the two most important commandments are to love God and to love others. He exemplified this in his life by leaving his throne in heaven to be born a human baby, with no bed and no home. He gave up his crown of glory for a crown of thorns, dying in our place so that we could live forever with him in paradise.

As teachers, it's all too easy to fall into the trap of "been there, done that" with kids—especially if you've been teaching for years. As you prepare for this week's lesson, remember that we can never know everything or be the best. Open your heart to God's will this week, with humility at your core. Let him teach you new ways to reach kids for his kingdom.

DEPARTURE PRAYER

(up to 5 minutes)

In this prayer, children discover that even though Jesus was strong and powerful, he was also gentle and kind.

Items to Pack:
1 copy per child of the "Face of Jesus" handout (at the end of this lesson), pens or pencils

Have children sit in a circle. Distribute pens or pencils and the "Face of Jesus" handout.

Say: **Close your eyes and imagine Jesus. Think of what we've read about Jesus in the Bible. Think of what you've learned about Jesus from others. Think of your relationship with him and what he means to you.**

Okay, now open your eyes. Take a minute to write down words you'd use to describe Jesus on your picture of Jesus.

Give children time to write descriptive words about Jesus on their handouts. If kids struggle to write, let them know they can draw pictures to describe him, too.

Ask: • **Tell about what you wrote or drew about Jesus.**

Let kids talk about the words they used to describe Jesus. You'll likely hear words like "strong" or "powerful" and "nice."

Say: **You have great words. Jesus is all of those things. Often when we think about Jesus, we think about all the amazing things he did, such as heal sick people, calm a storm, or come back to life. And Jesus is very strong and mighty. Jesus is also very gentle and kind. He cared for people and loved them, and he loves us today. Take one more minute to write two more words on your picture that describe Jesus. If you didn't have "gentle" and "loving," add those. Or you may have heard a word someone else used and want to add it.**

Give kids time to add extra words.

Say: **As you look at your picture, think of what Jesus means to you. Put your finger on one word or drawing from your picture. As I pray, we'll thank Jesus for all that he is. When I pause, think or say the word your finger is on. Let's all bow our heads.**

Pray: **Dear Jesus, thank you for all you do for us. You did amazing miracles in the Bible and you do wonderful things in our lives today. Thank you for being...**

Pause for kids to say or think their word.

Thank you for being an example of what it means to be gentle and loving. Thank you for paying the price for our sins so we can live with you in heaven forever. Help us to be more like you. In your name, amen.

(15 minutes)

Humble or Not?

In this experience, kids act out different situations, once without humility and once with.

Say: **Today's Beatitude says that God blesses those who are humble. Matthew 5:5 says, "God blesses those who are humble, for they will inherit the whole earth."**

Ask: • **Explain what you think the word *humble* means.**

• **Tell about a time you or someone you know was humble.**

Items to Pack:
scenes (provided in lesson) for kids to act out, written on index cards

Say: **Being humble means to put others first. We can put others first by being gentle and kind, just like Jesus.**

Ask: • **Tell about a time you won something, like a spelling bee or soccer game.**

• **Explain what it was like for you when you won.**

• **Now tell about a time you lost at something, such as a game or a contest.**

• **What was it like for you to lose?**

Say: **Winning is a lot more fun than losing. People cheer for you and you might even win a trophy or prize. Everyone likes to feel like they're number one.**

But what Jesus says about winning is different from what the world teaches us about winning. The world teaches us to be the best and to be number one. Jesus teaches us to be humble and put others first, because  **God will reward us in heaven.**

Of course we always want to do our best, but the important thing is remembering that all we _do_ and _have_ comes from God. God doesn't want us to brag or boast, but instead to be gentle and kind and to put others first. And make God number one.

Have kids form groups of about four. Ensure that groups are varied in age if you have mixed ages in your room. Say: **We're going to see what the difference is between humility and pride. Each group will get a scene to act out in two different ways. First, you'll make a plan and act out the scene by bragging and being full of pride. The second time, you'll make a plan and act out the same scene by being humble and putting others first.**

Give each group one of the following scenes:

• **One of you is the only person to get an A on the spelling test.**
• **Your soccer team just won the biggest game of the year.**
• **One of you just got chosen to be the lead in the school play.**
• **Your parents just bought one of you the newest video games.**
• **You found a $20 bill on the ground.**
• **Your group of friends is racing, and one of you wins the race.**

Give groups five minutes to plan and practice how they'll act out their scenes. Then gather everyone's attention.

FUN FACT

In ancient Olympic Games, winners weren't awarded medals, but a crown of olive branches. They'd return to their home in a chariot drawn by white horses. And in modern times, the last Olympic medals to be made entirely out of gold were awarded in 1912.

Say: **Let's take turns acting out the scenes. With your group, first act out your scene by bragging and being full of pride. The second time, be humble and kind. And be kind to other groups when it's their turn to act.**

Give each group one to two minutes to act out their scenes. Encourage kids to applaud one another. When each group has had a chance to act, bring everyone's attention back to you.

Say: **That was great!**

Ask: • **Describe whether you think it's okay for us to be proud of ourselves for doing something well.**

• **Why is it important to remember to be humble when we do well?**

Say: **It's okay to be proud of ourselves when we accomplish something. But we must listen to what Jesus said about how we act toward others. Jesus says it's more important to put others first than to be the best. We may not always win a trophy here on earth, but when we do what Jesus says,** **God will reward us in heaven.**

STORY EXCURSION

(10 minutes)

A Humble Servant

Kids learn how Jesus is our ultimate example of humility.

Say: **Let's dig into what God's Word says about being humble. I have Bible verses that explain more about being humble. We'll look for and read these verses together.**

Work together to find and read each of the Bible references. After you've read the verse, summarize it. The Scripture references and summaries are printed below for your convenience.

- 1 Peter 5:5—We are to serve each other in humility.
- Proverbs 11:2—Wisdom comes to those who are humble.
- Matthew 11:29—Jesus is humble and gentle.
- James 4:10—When we humble ourselves before God, he'll honor us.

Read aloud Philippians 2:5-11.

Ask: • **What does this passage about Jesus tell you about being humble?**

Items to Pack:
Bibles, large bowl of warm water, cup, paper towels

TOUR GUIDE TIP

Only have kids who want to read aloud do so; don't put a child on the spot to read to the rest of the group.

Say: **Jesus is the greatest example of humility. He left his heavenly kingdom to come to earth as a little human baby. Verse 7 says he took the humble position of a slave.**

Ask: • **What do you think of when you hear the word** *slave*?

• **What do you think it means that Jesus became a slave?**

Say: **A slave is someone who serves others or a master. Jesus was a slave to God and to people.**

Ask: • **How did Jesus serve God?**

• **How did Jesus serve people?**

• **Explain how you think God rewarded Jesus, based on this passage.**

Say: **Jesus served God by obeying him. Jesus died on the cross, like a criminal, even though he'd done nothing wrong. God rewarded Jesus in heaven, giving him the highest place of honor there. And every knee on earth will one day bow to Jesus and confess that he is king.**

Ask: • **How can we have the same attitude as Jesus?**

• **What ways can we serve God in daily life?**

• **What ways can we serve others?**

Say: **Jesus is God's Son. Jesus is the king of all kings—but he didn't come to be served and treated like a king. In fact, he did the exact opposite.**

Open your Bible to John 13:3-9. Say: **In this passage, Jesus took out a bowl of water. He began to wash the feet of his disciples. Imagine what a dirty job that was! In Bible times, the people didn't have socks and shoes or sidewalks like us. They wore sandals and walked in dirt and rocks. The disciples' feet must have been filthy and smelly! But still Jesus washed them, and even dried them with a towel he'd wrapped around his waist.**

When he was finished, Jesus explained what he'd done for his disciples. Even though they called him Teacher and Lord, he humbled himself by serving them and washing their feet. And Jesus told them to follow his example. He said, "I have given you an example to follow. Do as I have done to you."

Today, we're going to be like Jesus and serve one another. I'm not going to make you wash each other's feet. But we are going to take turns washing each other's hands.

FUN FACT

When Jesus and his disciples ate the Last Supper, they were actually celebrating the Jewish Feast of Passover. The second step in the Passover Seder is the washing of hands (*urchatz* in Hebrew). Jewish law required the washing of hands before dipping any food into liquid. It was at this point in the meal that Jesus went a step further and washed the disciples' feet.

Place the bowl of warm water and the cup in the center of the room, and put paper towels near the bowl. Have kids sit in a circle around the bowl.

Choose a child to begin, then say: **You're going to take turns washing one another's hands. Everyone will wash the hands of the person sitting on their right. Have the person on your right place his or her hands over the bowl. Use the cup to pour water over their hands. As you pour the water, say the first part of our Beatitude: "God blesses those who are humble." Then give the person a paper towel to dry with. When that person has finished drying, he or she can invite the next person up and wash that person's hands.**

Invite kids to come and wash each other's hands. Prompt them if they need help remembering to say, "God blesses those who are humble." When everyone's hands are washed, have kids sit back down in the circle.

Say: **Jesus is a king—yet he left his throne to come to our world to die for our sins. Because he was humble and obedient, God rewarded him by honoring him above everyone else. When we follow Jesus' example and humble ourselves by serving others, ◑ God will reward us in heaven.**

ADVENTURES IN GROWING

(15 minutes)
Humble Pie

Children eat miniature pies while learning about how God changes our hearts.

Say: **Today we're learning that ◑ God will reward us in heaven. Did you know that gentleness and kindness are Fruits of the Spirit?**

The Bible says that loving God produces "fruit" in our lives. This means that when we take what Jesus says into our hearts and learn to be more like him, the Holy Spirit will help us have characteristics of love, joy, peace, patience, kindness, goodness, faithfulness, gentleness, and self-control. These are called the Fruit of the Spirit.

◑ God will reward us in heaven, but on earth Jesus wants us to learn to be more like him. When we're more like Jesus, we put other people first.

Today we're going to make a very fruity snack to remind us to be more like Jesus. Our snack is called "humble pie."

Ask: **• Explain what you think humble pie is.**

Items to Pack:

sugar cookies or wafers; non-dairy whipped topping; assorted chopped fruit such as strawberries, kiwi, raspberries, and peaches; paper plates; plastic spoons

ALLERGY ALERT: Check with parents about allergies and dietary concerns, and post a copy of the "Allergy Alert" sign (at the end of this book) where parents will see it.

TOUR GUIDE TIP

Some children are allergic to dairy or certain types of fruit, so have an alternative snack for these kids.

Say: **To "eat humble pie" doesn't mean to eat a real pie. It's an expression that means to apologize for making a big mistake. It usually happens when we say something that we don't mean or doesn't come out right. Let me give you an example.**

Tell an appropriate example of a time you had to "eat humble pie." While it can be embarrassing to relive those moments, kids will get a kick out of hearing that their teacher makes mistakes, too.

Ask: • **Tell about a time you had to eat humble pie.**

• **Explain what it was like for you to have to apologize for a mistake you made.**

Say: **No one likes to feel embarrassed or ashamed. So I'll teach you a special secret for how to not have to eat humble pie—and it's really simple! If we put others before us, it'll keep us from making big mistakes and having to eat humble pie.**

We're going to make our own pies today for a snack. But they're not humble pies; they're Fruit of the Spirit pies that will remind us to be more like Jesus. The sugar cookie is your pie crust. I'll help you put whipped cream onto the cookie. Then you'll choose which fruits to put on top of the whipped cream.

Give each child a sugar cookie on a paper plate. Help kids spread the whipped cream on their cookie. Provide a variety of chopped fruits in bowls, and let kids spoon fruit onto the whipped cream-topped cookie. Then have kids sit and enjoy their snacks.

FUN FACT *Humble pie* is derived from "umble pie," which was an actual medieval meat pie usually served to servants. Umble pie was filled with the chopped innards of an animal, such as the heart, lungs, and kidneys. *Umble* comes from the term *nomble,* which is French for "deer's innards." Yum!

SOUVENIRS →

(10 minutes)

Inherit the Earth

In this experience, children imagine what awaits them in heaven.

Say: **Matthew 5:5 says that if we're humble, we will inherit the earth.**

Ask: • **What do you think Jesus meant by that?**

Say: **This earth isn't our home; it's just temporary. But Jesus promises that if we follow him, we'll live forever with him in the kingdom of heaven. Our reward isn't here on earth. When we're humble and put others first, 🥧 God will reward us in heaven.**

Turn to a partner and discuss these questions:

Ask: • **What do you imagine heaven looks like?**

Items to Pack:
Bible; 1 copy per child of the "Inherit the Earth" handout (at the end of this lesson) copied onto card stock; pens or pencils; glue; an assortment of craft supplies such as cotton balls, foil, ribbon, chenille wires, and sequins; Travel Journals; whiteboard and dry-erase marker (optional)

Some children may have a lot to say about heaven, while others may feel scared or have questions. If children have questions you can't answer, it's okay to say, "I don't know," or "That's a good question, I'll look for an answer this week." No one can know for sure what heaven looks like, but there are a lot of resources on the topic. For a more in-depth study on heaven, check out Group's *Heaven Is for Real* products at group.com.

Items to Pack:

Bibles, 1 copy per child of the "Be Like Jesus" handout (at the end of this lesson), 2 hand mirrors, dry-erase marker, assortment of over-sized clothes (such as shirts and jackets), baby clothes, baby powder, cradle (optional), bowl of toy fruit (preferably 9 pieces), sticky notes, pens, soft worship music, a music player

Ahead of time, prepare Travel Stops (prayer stations) so they're easy to set out when it's time for Home Again Prayer. Cut apart the sections on the "Be Like Jesus" handout and place each at the appropriate Travel Stop.

• **Why do you think being in heaven with Jesus is part of our reward?**

Give kids time to discuss, encouraging them to take turns speaking.

Say: **The Bible gives some descriptions of heaven. Let's read what the Apostle John saw.**

Read out loud Revelation 21:11-14.

Ask: • **What, if anything, surprised you about this description of heaven?**

Consider writing kids' answers on a whiteboard as a reminder while they're working on their Travel Journal pictures next.

Say: **Heaven sounds amazing, and this is just a glimpse of what it'll be like. We're going to use our imaginations to make pictures of heaven. Our papers have an award outline because ◗ God will reward us in heaven. Use whatever supplies you'd like to make your picture.**

Let kids draw pictures of heaven and decorate their pictures. When they're finished, set aside the pictures to dry. If the glue is dry by the end of class, store the pictures in their Travel Journals. If the glue is still wet, you may have to wait until next session to add them to the Travel Journals.

HOME AGAIN PRAYER

(up to 5 minutes)

Place the appropriate instructions, a Bible, and supplies at each Travel Stop. Set up each station as follows:

Travel Stop 1: On the mirrors, write JESUS using a dry-erase marker.

Travel Stop 2: Lay out an assortment of oversized clothes.

Travel Stop 3: Lay out baby clothes. If you have a manger or small cradle, place the clothes inside. Lightly sprinkle the clothes with baby powder so they smell like a real baby.

Travel Stop 4: Write one Fruit of the Spirit on each of nine sticky notes, and stick each one to a piece of toy fruit. (The Fruit of the Spirit is love, joy, peace, patience, kindness, goodness, faithfulness, gentleness, and self-control.) Place the fruit in a bowl or basket.

Open the Bible to Philippians 2:5.

Say: **Earlier we learned about having the same attitude as Jesus, one that's humble, gentle, kind, and loving; always putting others before ourselves.**

For our closing prayer, I've set up four different stops. Each one will challenge you to think of ways to live out what we've learned today. There are instructions at each stop. While I play the worship music, go to any of the stops and follow the instructions. You might have time to do all four stops or you may only get to do one; that's okay, take your time. Remember, this is prayer time. It's time for you to spend time talking with God, not with your friends.

Start the music and have children travel to the different stops. Walk around the room, helping kids who can't read and keeping kids on track. Depending on time or how children respond, you might play two songs. When the music stops, bring the kids back into a circle.

Say: **As we leave today, let's remember to humble ourselves like Jesus. And when we do, God will reward us in heaven. Let's bow our heads as I close in prayer.**

Pray: **Jesus, thank you for being obedient to God's call. Thank you for humbling yourself to die for our sins. Help us to be more like you. Open our eyes to see ways to put others first. Thank you for our reward in heaven. In your name, amen.**

SCENIC ROUTE →

If you don't have the time or space for the Travel Stop stations, close in prayer using only Travel Stop 1. Pass a mirror to each child, allowing him or her to look into it. As a group, discuss how others can see Jesus in you this week.

FACE OF Jesus

Inherit the Earth

Be Like Jesus

Directions: Cut apart the sections, and place each at the appropriate Travel Stop.

Read Philippians 2:5.

• Look in the mirror. What do you see?

• How can you ensure others see Jesus in you this week?

Put on a piece of clothing.

Read 1 Peter 5:5.

• The Bible tells us to imitate Jesus, which means we should act and talk like him.

• What's one way you can be like Jesus this week?

Read John 1:14.

• Pick up the baby clothes and look at them. Think about Jesus being a little baby.

• Say a prayer, thanking Jesus for leaving his home in heaven to become a humble baby on earth.

Read Galatians 5:22.

• Look through the bowl of fruit.

• Pick up the Fruit of the Spirit that you need more of in your life.

• Pray that God would help you show this fruit to others this week.

Journey 7

God Blesses Those Who Are Fair

Pathway Point: 🌀 God makes everything right.

In-Focus Verse: "God blesses those who hunger and thirst for justice, for they will be satisfied" (Matthew 5:6).

Travel Itinerary

Today's Scripture is one simple verse—but the reality of its impact has always been one that we struggle with. There are many things in life that aren't fair. And kids, who often think in black-and-white terms, often struggle with the issue of fairness as well.

At the moment Jesus proclaimed that blessed was the person who hungered and thirsted for justice, he knew the time was coming when he would be mocked, scorned, and vilified as the "King of the Jews." Jesus knew his time on earth was short and that the most difficult part of the journey would soon follow.

The unjust punishment, crucifixion, and burial of Jesus would leave a lasting impression on his followers. Although his torture and treatment was undeserved and bore no sense of fairness, God in his glory made all things right through the glorious resurrection. He did it for Jesus then; he does it for us now.

DEPARTURE PRAYER

(up to 5 minutes)

Children discover that even when life seems totally unfair, God will make all things right.

Items to Pack:

For each child: a gold-painted 1-inch section of a cardboard tube (from a paper towel roll), several sequins or small plastic jewels, half a shell from a large plastic Easter egg, and 1 battery-powered flameless votive candle

Also: Bible, glue, several pairs of scissors, 1 whole plastic Easter egg, half a plastic Easter egg shell, bowl, 1 completed crown sample (made prior to class), 1 battery-powered flameless votive candle

Say: **Jesus left his home in heaven, where he was a king.** Show kids the sample crown.

He came to earth as a fragile human being, just like you and me. Show kids the egg.

When people turned on Jesus, they hung him on a cross, and his body was broken. Mimic breaking the egg. **Jesus' life was poured out, much like I'm pouring out this egg.** Mimic emptying the egg into the bowl.

Ask: • **What do we usually do with broken eggshells?**

Say: **People planned to toss Jesus away, too, but God had another plan. God took Jesus' broken body and gave him back his heavenly crown.** Set the plastic eggshell half in the crown so it will hold the flameless votive candle.

FUN FACT

The Sermon on the Mount took place relatively early in Jesus' ministry, after he'd been baptized by John the Baptist and preached in Galilee.

FUN FACT

How much would the stone weigh that covered Jesus' tomb? Depending on the type of stone used, it could have weighed between 1 to 2 tons, or 2,000 to 4,000 pounds.

Say: **God made Jesus the light of the world.** Place the battery-powered flameless votive candle in the eggshell and turn it on.

God replaced Jesus' broken, empty shell with life and gave him power and authority. God wants us to share Jesus' light with others.

We're going to make these candle holders to remind us of what God did with Jesus' broken body to give us new life. This also reminds us that ◑ **God can make everything right for us just as he did for Jesus, his Son.**

Give each child supplies to make a crown candle holder. Kids can cut notches on one edge of the cardboard roll to create a crown and then glue on the decorations. Give kids each an eggshell half and a battery-powered flameless votive candle to set inside the crown. Set aside the crafts to dry.

Ask: • **Why do you think God allowed Jesus' body to be unfairly broken?**

• **What's important to you about Jesus coming back to life?**

• **How do you think God makes things right?**

Say: **We see lots of things in real life that don't seem fair.**

Ask: • **Tell about something unfair that happened to you or someone else.**

• **What was that experience like for you?**

Say: **As a young boy, Jesus already knew that his life and the way people treated him would be very unfair. Because Jesus was God's Son, he came into the world to fulfill his mission; he came to save us from our sins. Jesus didn't die for his own sins, because he lived a sinless life.**

Ask: • **Explain whether you think what happened to Jesus was fair.**

Say: **Jesus took this treatment for us because he wanted us to live with him forever in heaven, and he was willing to lay down his life for it. Jesus' faith that** ◑ **God would make things right was so strong, that even knowing he would be unfairly crucified didn't stop him from taking the unfair treatment.**

Let's ask God to help us know that even when life and people are unfair to us, ◑ **God makes everything right.**

Pray: **God, thank you for giving us Jesus' example to know that when we hunger and thirst for justice,** ◑ **God will make everything right. Help us remember that when we're unfairly treated, God in his goodness will provide justice for us. In Jesus' name, amen.**

1st STOP DISCOVERY

(15 minutes)

Sweet Justice

Kids will taste how God takes something bitter and makes it good.

Items to Pack:

Bible, small cups, unflavored soda water or club soda, white grape juice

ALLERGY ALERT ▶ Check with parents about allergies and dietary concerns, and post a copy of the "Allergy Alert" sign (at the end of the book) where parents will see it.

Ask kids to sit in a circle.

Say: **When Jesus was unfairly punished and crucified, his body was bruised, beaten, and bloodied.**

Imagine standing in the crowd and seeing Jesus this way. It would be hard to believe that God could make all things right at that moment. Even the people who'd followed Jesus and believed he was God's Son couldn't imagine that anything would ever be right again. All they had left was their faith in God that he would somehow take care of things.

Give kids each a cup half full of unflavored soda water, and tell them not to drink it.

Once everyone has a cup, say: **Go ahead and take a sip of your drink. Then turn to a partner and discuss what it tastes like.**

Allow time. Then ask for reports back to the entire group.

Say: **This drink wasn't very tasty. It was bitter and unpleasant.**

Add white grape juice to each cup to fill it. Once the cups are full, tell kids to taste the drink.

Ask: • **What happened to your unpleasant drink?**

• **Describe what's different about it now.**

• **Why do you think adding another ingredient changed it so much?**

• **How is this like what happens when something "bitter" happens in real life?**

Say: **Notice how the bad taste seemed to disappear and the drink became something tasty and sweet. When unfair or bitter things happen in our lives, we can have faith that God will take those things and make them right, just like the grape juice made the bitter soda water sweet.**

Our lives can be like bitter soda water without God. When we have faith in God, a change takes place. He takes the unfair and bad things that happen and, when we're faithful, ◗ God makes everything right.

Read aloud Matthew 5:6: **"God blesses those who hunger and thirst for justice, for they will be satisfied."**

TOUR GUIDE TIP Have a personal example ready to tell kids about how you've experienced God making things right in an unfair situation. Offering your personal experience draws in kids and models how they can share their thoughts and experiences with you.

Say: **If you experience bitter things that seem unfair or unjust, you can be reassured that God will make everything right.**

Okay, now it's your turn. Turn to a partner and tell about a time you or someone close to you was treated unfairly.

Allow one minute; then signal time for the other partner to talk. After one minute, gather kids' attention.

Say: **Sometimes those memories are unpleasant. Most of us have been treated unfairly at one time or another.**

Ask: • **Now tell your partner about a time when someone treated you fairly.**

Allow one minute; then signal time for the other partner to talk. After one minute, gather kids' attention. Ask for a few kids to share their experiences with the larger group.

Expect to hear about conflicts with parents, siblings, and friends, and sports-related incidents. Children will easily be able to relate situations regarding material things, but prompt them to also include emotional, spiritual, and social experiences that may have occurred, or offer your own.

Say: **Thanks for sharing your experiences.**

Ask: • **Why do you think it's important to stand up for what's right and fair?**

• **What happens if we choose not to stand up for what's right?**

• **Why do you think it matters to God if we stick up for what's right?**

Say: **Imagine what would've happened if Jesus hadn't been willing to stand up for us by going to the cross, even though we are still sinners!**

Open your Bible and read aloud Romans 6:22-23.

Say: **Jesus told us in Matthew 5:6 that those of us who seek justice will be satisfied because God makes everything right. We can have faith in that. Jesus was more than fair to us when he died for our sins on the cross; he paid unjustly for our sins. And God made everything right by bringing Jesus back to life and giving him the place of honor in heaven.**

(10 minutes)

Water at the Well

Kids experience what it's like to thirst for something.

Items to Pack:

Bible, pretzels, 2 buckets (with handles) filled ⅔ with water, towels in case of spills, 1 bucket for your demonstration of the lesson

ALLERGY ALERT ▶ Check with parents about allergies and dietary concerns, and post a copy of the "Allergy Alert" sign (at the end of this book) where parents will see it.

Have kids stand in a circle. Say: **Let's take an imaginary journey. Close your eyes. Imagine that you're walking in a hot, hot desert. Keep your eyes closed and turn to your right. Place one hand on the shoulder of the person in front of you. Now march—you'll walk around in a circle. Imagine you're walking in the desert. There's no breeze, and the sun is beating down on you. You feel little beads of sweat rolling down your face. You can feel it trickling down your back. Use your free hand to fan yourself.**

As you keep walking in the hot, hot sun, you realize your mouth is really dry. You haven't had a drink in hours. All you can think about now is a tall, cool drink of water—but there's no water. You keep walking, getter hotter and more thirsty and tired as you march along. Keep your eyes closed. It's hard to lift your feet to walk anymore, so just shuffle as you walk. You keep going, hoping against hope that you'll finally have your thirst satisfied when you drink that first swallow of cool, cool water. Swallow really hard. As you think about the deep thirst you feel, you're going to eat a dry, salty pretzel. Give each child a pretzel. **Keep your eyes closed and keep walking as you eat the pretzel. Feel how dry your mouth is, and imagine, one last time, how much you wish you could have a drink of that cool, cool water.**

Pause for one minute. Say: **Open your eyes.**

Ask: • **Describe what it's like to be very thirsty.**

• **How do you think that feeling is like how it feels to "thirst "for justice?**

• **Why do you think it matters to God if we thirst for justice?**

Say: **Thirsting for justice is a lot like how it feels to be thirsty for water. It's something you need, and you know how good you'll feel to taste that water. Seeing an unfair situation made right is like that first taste of water—it's refreshing and soothing.**

We're lucky to be able to go to the faucet and have fresh water! Think about how many times a day you use fresh water in your daily life. We use it all the time—for drinking, washing our bodies,

TOUR GUIDE TIP

If you have kids who are younger or who can't manage the bucket alone, let kids partner up.

brushing our teeth, doing laundry—there are all kinds of ways we use water every single day.

Now imagine how different our lives would be if we couldn't go to a faucet to get water. Imagine if you only had a chance to drink fresh water a few times a week or if you could only bathe in water a few times a month. That would be really hard.

Ask: • **What kinds of things would you have to do without?**

Say: **During Jesus' day, it wasn't easy to get water. People didn't have sinks or tubs. People would go to the well to get their water. Let's see what that might be like.**

Use the bucket to demonstrate scooping water from a well as described.

Say: **People had to reach way down deep and pick up water from the bottom of the well. If they needed a lot of water, they had to fill up many buckets to carry home. They might live far away from the well, and it might have been a long and hard trip to collect the water and make it back home with those very heavy buckets that were now splashing and full.**

Let's try this ourselves to see how hard it was to get water from the well and then make it back home.

Have kids form two groups. Send groups to opposite sides of the room.

Explain to kids that they'll hurry with a full bucket of water from one end of the room to the other and then hand off the bucket to the next person in line until everyone has had a chance to participate.

Say: **There's just one catch. During this challenge, not one tiny bit of water can spill or splash on the floor, so you must be very careful as you walk back and forth.**

Let kids play, taking care to clean up any spills with the towels.

Ask: • **What was that experience like for you?**

• **What was it like to struggle to move the water?**

• **Tell whether this experience changed how you value water, and explain why or why not.**

Say: **During Jesus' time, water was a precious resource. Today it's also a precious resource—we can't live without it! Although it's more readily available to us today, in many places in the world people still struggle daily to get water. One day long ago, Jesus encountered a woman sitting at a well who was fetching water. It was tiring work.**

Open your Bible and read aloud John 4:13.

Say: **At first the woman at the well didn't understand what Jesus was saying to her, but after talking with him, she began to understand that he was talking about more than just her earthly thirst for water.**

When we follow Jesus, he'll take care of our physical needs for food and water, and he'll quench our thirst for justice when things are unfair. We can stay focused on God and not on the things in this world.  **God will make everything right.**

SOUVENIRS →

(10 minutes)

Everlasting Water

Children decorate water bottles to remind them of God's promise to satisfy their thirst.

Items to Pack:
1 water bottle for each child (available online or at discount stores), permanent markers in a variety of colors, 1 index card per child with Matthew 5:6 (verse and reference) written on it

Have kids form pairs. Distribute the water bottles, permanent markers, and a copy of the Scripture to each set of partners.

Say: **We're going to spend time now creating a reminder of how** **God makes everything right. You can take your water bottle with you everywhere you go. Spend time decorating it and include the Scripture from the card, our Beatitude for today's lesson: "God blesses those who hunger and thirst for justice, for they will be satisfied" (Matthew 5:6). As you work, discuss the following questions with your partner.**

Ask: **• Tell about a time you experienced something really unfair. What did you do?**

• Tell about a time you stood up for something right, even though it wasn't the popular choice.

• This water bottle can travel with you wherever you go, and God is always with you. How does knowing God is always there for us help you face unfair or unjust situations?

Allow time for kids to work together and discuss the questions. Then gather their attention back to you.

Say: **As we take our water bottles with us and drink from them, we can be reminded that only Jesus can provide the living water that we need to live a life that is just and right.**

Jesus is not saying that life will always be fair and right, but when we follow him and believe in him, he can make everything right.

TOUR GUIDE TIP

Let children work in pairs so they can grapple with the questions in this section together.

Items to Pack:

1 copy per child of the "God Makes Everything Right" handout (at the end of this lesson), pencils, soft praise music, music player, Travel Journals

TOUR GUIDE TIP

If you have younger kids who can't write, partner them with an older child for assistance.

HOME AGAIN PRAYER

(up to 5 minutes)

Distribute pencils and copies of the "God Makes Everything Right" handout to kids, along with their Travel Journals.

Say: **The purpose of this handout is for you to create your own record of how God makes things right in your everyday life. As you go to school, play with your friends, and share daily life with your family, you can record how God helps you by making things right. In the column on the left, you can record a challenge, problem, or unfair situation. It's okay to write it down or draw it. Then you can pray to God about the situation. Watch carefully and see what happens. Over time, you'll be able to record in the right column how God helped you and made everything right. Things may not turn out the way you want or expect them to, but in the end we know God knows his plans for us. We can't always see the big picture...but this record can help us get a glimpse of God working on our behalf.**

Tell kids they'll start today by thinking about a situation they're facing that seems problematic or unfair. They can write or draw it on the page and then take a few moments to pray to God about it. When kids have finished, have them place their handouts in their Travel Journals. Let kids know that anytime they see God make things right or they face an unfair situation, they can add that to the page.

Turn on the praise music, and allow about five minutes for kids to work. Collect the Travel Journals, and put them away till next week.

Say: **We've talked a lot about how God wants us to stand up for what's right and how even in situations that are unfair, we can have faith that 🌎 God makes everything right. Let's take time to pray together about what we've learned today. You can pray out loud or silently. Please join me in kneeling on the floor.**

Pause as children kneel with you in prayer.

Say: **I'll begin. Please join me.**

Pray: **God, we thank you today that you're our great provider. We praise you and thank you for all the ways you take care of us. Please hear our prayer as we pray together.**

God, thank you for providing us with food and water. Thank you for helping us stand up for what's right. Thank you for making us hunger and thirst for what's right and for justice. Only you can

quench our thirst. Please help us do what's fair and just in our lives by following your example. We now silently ask you to help us follow your will. We know ● you will make everything right. Hear our prayers as we ask you to make us more like you every day.

Pause so children can complete their prayers.

Pray: **In Jesus' name, amen.**

God Makes Everything Right

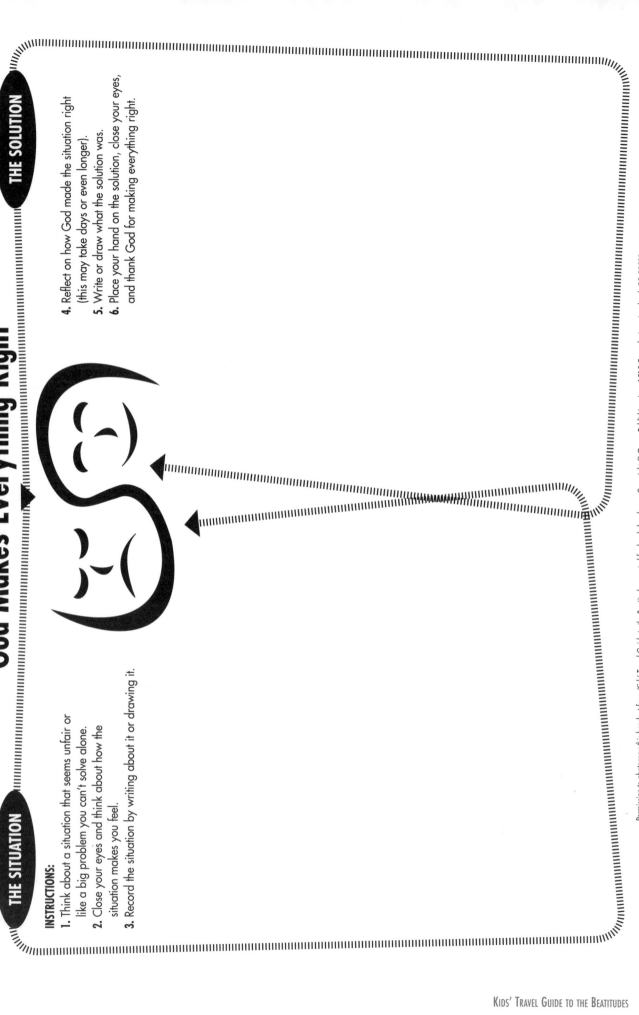

4. Reflect on how God made the situation right (this may take days or even longer).
5. Write or draw what the solution was.
6. Place your hand on the solution, close your eyes, and thank God for making everything right.

THE SITUATION

INSTRUCTIONS:

1. Think about a situation that seems unfair or like a big problem you can't solve alone.
2. Close your eyes and think about how the situation makes you feel.
3. Record the situation by writing about it or drawing it.

God Blesses Those Who Are Merciful

Pathway Point: 🌐 God is kind to us.

In-Focus Verse: "God blesses those who are merciful, for they will be shown mercy" (Matthew 5:7).

Travel Itinerary

God doesn't play fair—and that's reason for praise!

We don't deserve God's mercy. Every human who's ever lived has totally blown it in regard to God's holy standards. By a strict standard of justice, we should all be doomed.

So God, in overflowing love for the world he created, showed us mercy when he sent his one and only Son, Jesus, to live, die, and come back to life...in our place, to pay our overwhelming sin debt.

If that weren't already more than enough, God sent his Spirit into the world to nudge us, sheep that we are, to acknowledge our sin and our need for a Savior.

Hallelujah, God has mercy! God doesn't give us what we deserve—eternal death—but instead gives us what we don't deserve—eternal life in heaven with Jesus. God is definitely kind to us.

Jesus' reference to mercy in the Beatitudes would've recalled for his audience the prophet Micah's exhortation to follow in God's good example to act justly, love mercy, and walk humbly with him (Micah 6:8). God has shown us mercy and expects his people to extend mercy to others.

Ouch.

We like a fair game, evenly-sized pieces of pie, and for the good guy to win the day. The bad guy deserves to be locked up and the key tossed into a deep swamp.

Right?

Jesus turns our expectations upside-down. Because we have received mercy, we can extend mercy; then, when we need it, mercy will again be extended to us. It's not easy, but it's the better way.

To whom do you need to extend mercy? Allow the truth of this verse to flow into your life this week and you will have more of God's blessings to share with others, including your kids.

Items to Pack:

Bibles, timer or stopwatch

FUN FACT
The word *beatitude* comes from the Latin *beatitudo*, meaning "blessedness."

DEPARTURE PRAYER

(up to 5 minutes)

In this prayer activity, children discover that God shows mercy—and they can, too.

Ask kids to find a partner. Distribute a Bible to each pair.

Say: **The person whose birthday is closest to today goes first. Hold your arms out straight, palms up. When I say "go," your partner will place a Bible on your palms. Your job is to hold it up without bending your arms for as long as you can. I'll time you and let you know each time 10 more seconds have passed. If you feel like you can't hold your arms up any longer, call "Mercy!" to your partner. That will signal your partner to put his or her arms under yours to help you. Let's see if we can each make it to one minute.**

Do the challenge once, and then repeat as partners trade roles. If time permits, let kids try a few more times, adding a second Bible or seeing who can last the longest without calling for mercy. Afterward, have kids sit in a circle.

Ask: • **How might this experience have been different if you didn't know your partner would help you?**

• **What if you called "Mercy!" and your partner didn't help you?**

• **Tell about a time you needed help and someone helped you.**

Say: **Let's stop here and thank God for helping us all the time when we need it most. I'll start and you can jump in.**

Pray: **Dear God, thanks for giving us life and giving us friends to help us live well. Thank you for helping me when...** (add your own example, and pause while kids pray). **God, help us to become even better at helping others today. In Jesus' name we pray, amen.**

Ask: • **When you needed help in this challenge, you called "Mercy!" How would you explain to someone else what "mercy" means?**

Say: **Sometimes life gets hard and we need others to help us, to show us mercy as they hold us up in ways we can't hold ourselves up. God shows us mercy in so many ways, and he wants us to be merciful, too.**

1st STOP DISCOVERY

(15 minutes)

Begging for Mercy

Kids imagine an experience that illuminates God's mercy.

Items to Pack:
Bible

Say: **Mercy is helping people who can't help themselves. It's being kind to someone who might not expect it, deserve it, or even know they need your kindness.**

Jesus showed mercy to people even when others thought he shouldn't. We're going to learn about a situation where Jesus helped someone who was blind. Close your eyes. Imagine your world has gone totally dark. We don't know if the blind man in this story was born blind or something later in life made him blind. Turn to someone next to you and, without opening your eyes, tell them which you'd prefer: to never have the gift of sight or to have sight but then lose it later. Allow time.

Ask: • **What was it like for you to talk with your partner without your sight?**

Say: **Let's find out what happened. I'm going to read to you. When I say something the blind man said, I want you to repeat it after me—but remember, keep your eyes closed! Let's practice: "The blind man began shouting, 'Jesus, Son of David, have mercy on me!' "** (Pause while kids shout the line—and try it again if they didn't respond enthusiastically.)

Great job! So for now your eyes can't see, but your imagination can. Let your imagination take you into this situation. Hear it, smell it, feel it under your fingers, put yourself in the place of this man who can't use his eyes for information. Ready?

Read Luke 18:35-43, pausing to let kids repeat the blind man's words in verses 38-39 and 41. If you've turned out all the lights, turn them on again before verse 41.

Say: **You can see! Stand so you can follow Jesus! Celebrate! Praise God! Tell others so they will praise God, too!** Encourage kids to celebrate for about 30 seconds, and then ask them to be seated.

Ask: • **Why do you think the blind man shouted for Jesus?**

• **This man was willing to make a spectacle to get Jesus' attention. What do you think that says about his faith in Jesus?**

• **Who do you think showed mercy in this situation, Jesus or the crowd, and in what way?**

TOUR GUIDE TIP

If you can, make your meeting space as dark as possible for this experience, and read the Bible story by flashlight. Eliminating ambient light will further kids' ability to imagine blindness.

FUN FACT

Eighty percent of the information we gather through our senses comes through our eyes, so "turning off" that sense can help us experience things very differently.

• **How might this situation have turned out differently—for example, what if the blind man hadn't called to Jesus?**

Say: **Jesus showed mercy to the blind man. Jesus was kind to him, just like** 🌐 **God is kind to us. The blind man knew what his need was—he needed to see, and he needed God's mercy. The crowd needed Jesus' mercy, too, but they didn't seem to know it. Just like the blind man, we need God's mercy—often when we don't even realize it.**

STORY EXCURSION

(10 minutes)

Kindness in Action

This experience helps kids think about and put into action ways they can share mercy.

Ask kids to form groups of two or three, and give each group paper and pen.

Say: **Let's review what Jesus said again: "God blesses those who are merciful, for they will be shown mercy" (Matthew 5:7). In other words, people who give mercy get mercy in return.**

With your group, make a list of all the ways you can think of that God is kind to us. You'll have one minute to make your list as long as you can, and then we'll take turns creating a master list up front with no repeats. One minute begins...now!

When time's up, invite a child from the group closest to the poster board to write one thing from their list. Move clockwise around the room with each group adding something to the master list with no repeats. Continue around the room until every kindness is on the list. Give God a great big round of applause for all his tremendous acts of mercy.

Say: 🌐 **God is so kind to us—and he wants us to follow his example and be kind, too. Ready for round two? Flip over your paper and this time make a list of ways kids can be kind to others. Ready, go!**

After another minute, move counter-clockwise around the room to make a master list of kid kindnesses.

Say: **It's time for round three. With your group, look over this list of kid kindnesses and choose one thing your group can do in one minute or less for another group of kids in this room. You have one minute to create a plan. Go!**

After one minute, have groups each do their act of kindness for others and then be seated again.

Items to Pack:

paper, pens, poster board, markers, stopwatch or timer

TOUR GUIDE TIP

When kids are forming groups, encourage mixed ages so older and younger kids are in the same group. This offers a richer learning experience for younger kids, and gives older kids opportunities to take on leadership roles in small-group settings.

FUN FACT

Some research suggests that *acting* kind, even when one doesn't feel like *being* kind, improves a person's overall well-being. In other words, kindness has a boomerang effect: good for others, good for you!

Ask: • **Share something that stands out to you from the list of God's kindnesses, and explain why.**

• **What was it like to share kindness with someone just now?**

• **What's one thing you can do this week to be kind to others?**

If your group is primarily younger kids, highlight a few easy-to-do items on the kid kindness master list and have groups choose one.

(15 minutes)

Helpers in Motion

Children help others enjoy a snack.

Form two groups.

Say: **This is your team. With your team, think of people who are "helpers"—or people who help other people. It could be someone like a policeman or firefighter or doctor. Then think of a motion you can act out as a group to help the other team guess who your helper is. You have two minutes to come up with three helper people and motions.**

Starting with the team wearing the most green, take turns having teams act out one of their helpers while the other team guesses. Then have kids sit.

Ask: • **What was it like to "move" like your helper?**

• **When have you moved like one of the helpers your team chose?**

• **Why do you think God wants us to be helpers for others?**

Say: **People who help others are all around us. We all need help in life, and we can all give others help who need it.**

Ask for two willing kids to look up and read aloud Psalm 116:5 and Matthew 5:7. Before kids read the verses aloud, instruct the group to listen for what's similar and what's different about what the verses say. Let your readers repeat the verses if the group needs to hear them again.

Ask: • **Describe what's similar about these two Bible verses. What's different?**

Say: **God shows us mercy. God helps us and ◗ is kind to us. He blesses us as we follow his example and show mercy to others. Let's practice showing mercy now.**

Direct kids' attention to the snack and invite them to line up to receive it. As the first child takes a snack, say: **Wait! There's a condition to having today's snack. You can't eat the snack I give you. Instead, your job is to find someone else to serve your snack to.** Begin serving, and guide younger kids to serve others as needed.

Items to Pack:

Bibles, snacks in individual serving sizes

ALLERGY ALERT ▸ Check with parents about allergies and dietary concerns, and post a copy of the "Allergy Alert" sign (at the end of this book) where parents will see it.

TOUR GUIDE TIP

Your group may have a variety of reactions to the condition of snack time, from joy at a different experience to frustration because they're hungry. That's okay. Let them work through it and use it as a teachable moment.

TOUR GUIDE TIP

If your group is primarily older kids, have them discuss these questions in their groups. Give them a few minutes to talk, and then ask one child from each group to share something interesting from their discussion.

Items to Pack:

1 Bible and 1 dictionary for every group of kids, 1 copy per child of the "Defining Mercy" handout (at the end of this lesson), pens, Travel Journals

When everyone has a snack, ask: • **What was it like to trust that if you gave away your snack, someone else would give you his or hers?**

• **How is this experience like the verses we just read about mercy?**

• **How could real life be different if you looked out for ways you could help others and show mercy?**

Say: ◕ **God is kind to us all the time. He gives us life, our families and homes, friends and helpers, and an invitation to the adventure of being good helpers to others. We can be merciful just like God is merciful.**

SOUVENIRS →

(10 minutes)

Defining Mercy

Kids work to understand what mercy is all about as they add to their Travel Journals.

Distribute the Travel Journals, and then have kids form groups of three or four. Give each group a Bible and dictionary, and distribute handouts and pens. Say: **Let's take another look at mercy. Work together to look up Psalm 86:15 and read it aloud with your group. Then take turns looking up the four key words listed on your handout, and use your own words to create simple definitions. Then, look up and read Matthew 5:7. You have five minutes.**

When time's up, say: **With the definitions of the key words in mind, rewrite Psalm 86:15 and Matthew 5:7 in your own words.**

Allow time, and then ask a representative from each group to read their versions of the two verses.

Ask: • **What did you learn about God from taking a closer look at the key words in both verses?**

• **What do these verses tell us about how God wants his people to act?**

• **Turn to your group and tell about a time you were quick to get angry.**

• **How is being quick to get angry different from showing mercy?**

Say: **Some people seem to have more patience than others. But God wants his people to grow to be like him, full of compassion, mercy, patience, love, and faithfulness.** Add the handout to the Travel Journals and then collect the Travel Journals, putting them away till next week.

(up to 5 minutes)

Children thank God for his mercy.

Items to Pack:

Say: **Traditionally when someone approaches a king or queen, that person does something to show respect.**

Ask: • **Explain what people do when they come to talk to a king or queen.**

Pause to allow kids to respond.

Say: **They don't make eye contact, they bow low, and maybe they kneel or even get completely flat on the floor.**

Ask: • **Why do you think people do that?**

Say: **All those body postures are a sign of respect. The king or queen is in charge, and the people approaching the royal person are not, so they put their bodies lower than the royal person to show their place in life: lower than royalty. The king or queen is showing mercy to even allow a regular person to come into their presence, let alone to speak.**

But get this—God is the King of all kings, and he welcomes us into his presence. We can come to God whenever we want to and say whatever we want and it's all okay. That's pretty amazing.

Still, we want to show God respect and thank him for his great mercy. Right now, let's spread out around the room and assume a respectful body posture as if you were getting low before God: bow, kneel, lie flat, place your body however you'd like in order to show God respect. Allow time.

To show respect to God and thank God for his kindness to us, we're going to pray while you hold that position. I'll lead, but you'll have a chance to pray, too. Please pray with me.

Pray: **God, you are king and you are in charge. Please hear us as we recognize the way you show us mercy and grant us your many kindnesses.**

If you'd like to pray out loud, please do so now.

Pause so children can pray.

Pray: **God, you are merciful. Thank you for**  **being so kind to us. You invite us to be merciful and kind just as you are. Please hear us as we ask for your help to be kind to others.**

Please pray silently now, asking God to help you be kind and merciful to others.

Pause so children can pray.

Pray: **God, help others to see you through our acts of kindness. In Jesus' name, amen.**

DEFINING Mercy

Compassion _____

Mercy _____

Unfailing _____

Faithfulness _____

Psalm 86:15

Matthew 5:7

God Blesses Those Whose Hearts Are Pure

Pathway Point: ● God helps us know him.

In-Focus Verse: "God blesses those whose hearts are pure, for they will see God" (Matthew 5:8).

Travel Itinerary

God himself has come to earth—behold, Jesus our Savior!—and he brings in tow a new reality, a new way of living.

But while the Beatitudes may look in some ways like a checklist for good behavior in God's kingdom, this life isn't possible through our own efforts. It's only possible as God works in and through his people.

How many may have looked at this "list" (or others like it in the Bible), thought, *That'll never be me*, and sadly walked away from faith? Please be careful to not communicate that children need to "live better." Of course our choices are important—but they're only part of the story. God's grace covers all who call on the name of his Son.

And of course that's the best news of this Beatitude: God helps us know him! As we set our broken lives before him, confessing our sins and our need for God, God reveals himself to us.

What sins might be getting in the way of your relationship with God? As you prepare to teach this lesson, spend time in prayer. Ask him to show you any sin in your life that you need to hand over; ask him to make your heart pure. Spend time enjoying your relationship with God—and you'll be much better equipped to introduce others to him.

DEPARTURE PRAYER (up to 5 minutes)

In this prayer, children learn that God wants to know them.

Items to Pack:
none

Say: **I'm so pleased to see you all today. I look forward to getting to know you better as we journey together through today's Beatitude.**

Right now, let's make sure we all know everyone. Stand up, shake hands, and exchange a greeting with as many people as you can in the next minute. Especially try to meet anyone you haven't met before.

Items to Pack:

Bible; 2 clear pitchers of water; 1 long-handled spoon; 1 clear, empty filtration pitcher (available at discount and kitchen supply stores); 1 small cup full of potting soil; small cups, adult assistant

When time's up, ask: • **Describe what you usually say and do when you meet someone for the first time.**

• **When you're first getting to know someone, what kinds of things do you like to do together?**

• **Turn to someone next to you and share about when you first met someone you now consider to be a good friend.**

Say: **In order to have a good friend, you have to meet the person and get to know him or her first. Now consider that God wants to be your very good friend. Maybe there are people in this room who haven't met God yet. Prayer is one way to meet God and get to know him. Let's begin our time today by saying hello to God and asking him to help us get to know him better.**

Hold your right hand out like you're going to shake hands, and while I pray, imagine you're shaking hands with God. He's right here, you know, and he's really happy to meet you.

Let's pray:

Pray: **Good morning, God! (say it with me: Good morning, God!)**

We're so glad to be here with you today, and we're grateful that you want to help us know you better. Give us open minds, hearts, eyes, and ears, to see you and know you more. Thanks for everything, especially for being with us now and forever. In Jesus' name, amen!

(15 minutes)

Pure Living Water

In this experience, kids discover what "pure" looks like.

Have kids gather around you, and as they watch, pour the cup of dirt into one of the pitchers of water and use the spoon to stir it up. (Potting soil works really well.) Do this without commenting. Then begin pouring water into small cups, some from the pitcher of clean water and some from the pitcher of dirty water.

Say: **Water is essential to our bodies. Did you know that more than half of your body is made up of water? Most grown-ups could probably last a few days without food, but we would still need to drink water to live.**

Ask another adult to help you distribute cups of water to kids, some clean and some dirty.

Say: **We're distributing cups of water, but don't drink yet.**

When everyone has a cup, say: **Alright—ready to drink up?** Expect some kids to respond with confusion or disgust. **Not all of you look enthusiastic. You know you need water, right? It's good for you. So what's wrong?** Allow a few responses. **Oh...you don't want your cup of water? Would you like to trade it for another? If you'd like to trade, bring your cup here.**

As kids bring their cups forward, have them pour their dirty water into the empty filter pitcher. Offer them a cup of water from the clean pitcher instead. Accept all trades; depending on how dirty the dirty water looks, some kids might want to trade just because they're unsure whether their water came from the clean or the dirty pitcher.

When kids have emptied their cups into the filtration pitcher, gather your group around the filtration pitcher, remove the top, and show them the dirt collecting in the filter. As needed, add more water from the dirty pitcher.

Ask: • **What do you see happening to the water as it goes through the filter pitcher?**

Invite a willing child to read aloud Matthew 5:8.

Ask: • **What do you think it means to have a "pure heart"?**

• **How might a pure heart be like pure water?**

• **How is God like our filter to have a pure heart?**

Say: **If you'd like a refill of pure water, come on up. You'll need your cup full for what's next.**

Fill up kids' cups with clean water, and take a full cup for yourself.

Say: **I'm going to read to you an event from Jesus' life. Every time you hear the words "water," "drink," or "spring," take a sip.**

Read John 4:7-14 and John 7:37-38. Stop to take a sip from your cup each time you read "water," "drink," or "spring."

Say: **Jesus is sitting at a well when a woman comes up to fill her bucket with water. Jesus is a Jew and the woman is a Samaritan, and Jews and Samaritans don't like each other. Imagine if people from** [your state] **and** [neighboring state] **had been in a feud for so long that nobody can remember how it started but they know they aren't supposed to like each other.**

Jesus asks the woman for a drink, and then he tells her she should ask him for "living water."

Ask: • **Explain what you think living water might be.**

 Depending on how many kids you expect, you might have an additional clear pitcher of clean water available to fill kids' cups.

Say: **Jesus says this living water becomes like a bubbling spring within us, giving us eternal life. He also says anyone who believes in him may have a drink from it.**

Pour any dirty water left in the unclean pitcher into the filter pitcher.

Say: **Jesus wants us to believe in him because he is the way to a relationship with God, something pure like a bubbling spring that'll flow throughout our lives all the way into eternity. 🌐 God wants to help us know him. He wants to pour his love, his goodness, his life into our lives. Take a big sip to celebrate this great news: cheers!**

STORY EXCURSION

(10 minutes)

Pure Prayer

Kids spend time praying to get to know God better.

Have kids form groups of four as you distribute cups of your snack item and napkins to everyone. Ask kids to refrain from eating yet.

Say: **🌐 God wants to help us know him, and one way to get to know someone is to spend time talking together.**

Ask: • **What do you think God might want to talk about with you?**

As children call out responses, write them on the poster board where everyone can see. In case kids don't mention the following, you can offer a few suggestions: God wants to hear what we're thankful for, what we think we need, how we've messed up or need to grow and change, and what we really like about God.

Say: **Let's choose four of these responses and assign them to the colors (or shapes) of our snack.**

Make it clear by writing on the poster board what color or shape goes with which prayer category.

Say: **Okay, now we're going to spend time talking with God in our groups. Here's how it'll work. Open your napkin out flat so you have four squares. Starting with the person wearing the most red, choose one cracker from your cup, and pray based on the corresponding color (or shape).** It'll help to give an example based on what categories and colors kids decided. **Then put that cracker down in one square on your napkin. The next person can choose any cracker from their snack, pray, and put it in a square on their napkin. Continue around the circle until everyone has prayed through all the crackers and you each have four piles of crackers separated into "prayer" colors (or shapes).**

Items to Pack:

crackers or another snack that has four or more different colors or shapes, small disposable cups, napkins, poster board, tape, marker

ALLERGY ALERT ▶ Check with parents about allergies and dietary concerns, and post a copy of the "Allergy Alert" sign (at the end of this book) where parents will see it.

FUN FACT

While many adults feel uncomfortable praying out loud, children who are encouraged to pray aloud from an early age won't develop that same insecurity— so encourage away, but don't pressure.

TOUR GUIDE TIP

If your group is primarily younger kids, give more direction during this prayer experience. For example, have everyone choose a red fish and pray for that category first. You might consider going around the circle only once, maybe twice, but kids can still sort their snack.

Depending on the age of your group, either discuss the following questions as an entire group, or let kids discuss them in groups while they eat.

Ask: • **Explain what this prayer experience was like for you.**

• **How could praying help you know God better?**

• **If you set a time and place to regularly spend time with God in prayer, when and where would that be?**

If children discussed in small groups, ask willing kids to share highlights from their conversations.

Say: **Thanks for praying together. I know your prayers make God happy. Remember to pray often because God wants to help you know him.**

Items to Pack:
Bible, poster board, markers, age-appropriate magazines, glue sticks, several pairs of scissors

---

ADVENTURES IN GROWING

(15 minutes)
Picture a Pure Heart

Children create a collage to demonstrate pure living.

Give each child access to at least one magazine and pair of scissors. Ask for a willing child to read Matthew 5:8 aloud.

Say: **The pure in heart will be blessed because they get to see God! That's a pretty amazing promise. I want to be pure in heart, don't you? But what might it look like to be pure in heart? Let's search together for pictures that could be examples of living a pure life. We'll create a collage on this poster board that we can hang in our meeting space this month to remind us to be pure in heart.**

Let a child write the words "Pure in Heart Living" somewhere on the poster board. As kids flip through magazines and suggest pictures, have them explain to the group why they think particular pictures qualify. Keep an open mind as suggestions may vary widely, from a picture of someone exercising (the pure in heart take good care of the bodies God gave them) to a picture of cute animals (the pure in heart love all God's creatures). Encourage each child to select at least one picture and glue it to the poster board. When kids finish the collage, let children help you hang it up and give themselves a round of applause—they've got a blueprint for becoming pure in heart!

TOUR GUIDE TIP

If you have more than 12 children, do this activity in two or more groups. It'll help to have an adult in each group.

TOUR GUIDE TIP

If your children are older, have them write a description of why their picture fits as they add it to the collage. For younger children, you can write the description.

TOUR GUIDE TIP

Children can also do this activity at home with a parent's help or in small groups with an adult leader's help.

SOUVENIRS →

(10 minutes)

Just Add Jesus

This activity helps kids see the difference Jesus can make in their lives.

Ask kids to form groups of four to six. Distribute a "Just Add Jesus" handout to each person and have a willing child collect the supplies their group will need.

Say: **We're going to do an experiment. With an adult's help, follow the directions on your handout. We'll talk about what you discover when everyone's done.**

After groups have completed their experiment, ask kids to share highlights from the experience.

Ask: • **Explain what this experience was like for you.**

• **How is this experience like or unlike what happens when we rely on God to help us through our problems?**

Say: 🌐 **God helps us know him. He sent his Son, Jesus, to pay the price for our messes and to clean up our lives. We can't live better on our own without God's help. When we let God add more Jesus to our lives—by us believing in Jesus, telling him our sins, spending time with God in prayer and worship—** 🌐 **God helps us know him better and better. What a great gift!**

HOME AGAIN PRAYER

(up to 5 minutes)

Ask kids to spread out so they're not sitting immediately near one another enough to be distracted. Give a marker to each child.

Say: **We're going to spend time in quiet prayer with our eyes open.**

I'm going to read aloud a few verses from the Bible. As you listen, think about what you've learned today, that 🌐 **God helps us know him. Afterward, you'll have some quiet time to think about things you've done, words you've said, or thoughts you've had that might not be pure like God wants in us. For example, maybe you said something unkind to someone in your family or walked away from someone at school who was trying to be nice. For each thing you think of, use the marker to draw a dot on the palm of your hand. If you're like**

me, you might have quite a few dots—we all need God's help more than we think we do! Don't worry about going home a mess, though. We'll get you cleaned up before it's time to go.

Read Psalm 24:3-5 slowly and clearly.

Say: **Only those whose hands and hearts are pure will receive God's blessing and have a right relationship with him. So spend some quiet time thinking and drawing dots to demonstrate what you need to talk to God about. After you've made your dots, spend time talking to God about those things.**

When you think your group has had enough quiet time, say: **Only those whose hands and hearts are pure will receive God's blessing and have a right relationship with him. When you're done drawing dots on your hand, come to the front and kneel. I'll give you a wipe you can use to clean your hands, just like God cleans your heart.**

When all children are kneeling and have clean hands, pray out loud:

Pray: **Thank you, God, for giving us clean hands and pure hearts. We want to see you. We want your blessing on our lives. We want a right relationship with you. Thank you for forgiveness. Thank you that you know us inside and out and** **you want to help us know you. What a gift—a relationship with you, the One who made us and everything we see. Help us to know you and love you more every day. In Jesus' name, amen.**

Have kids throw their used wipes in the trash can.

Consider playing a quiet song of confession, familiar to your group, in the background while kids pray.

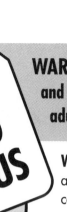

JUST ADD JESUS

WARNING! Because you'll be using food coloring, which can stain, and bleach, a potentially dangerous chemical, you must have an adult's help with this experiment.

What you'll need: This handout, Bible, a clear glass filled with water, food coloring, a plastic spoon, a medicine dropper, and a few drops of bleach. Have the adult carry the bleach and food coloring and be in charge of it during this experiment.

DIRECTIONS:

1. Set the glass of water between yourself and this handout. Read Matthew 5:8 through the water. If you're doing this with others, make sure everyone gets a turn.
2. Discuss:
   • What was it like to read through the glass of water?
3. Take turns and let everyone add one drop of food coloring to the water. Stir gently after each addition. Add at least 3 to 5 drops of food coloring; more is okay.
4. Try again to read Matthew 5:8 through the glass of water.

5. Discuss:
   • What was it like trying to read the verse through the water after adding the food coloring?
   • What things might get in the way of a pure relationship with God?
6. Spend a silent moment in prayer, telling God the things you want him to fix in your life.
7. Open your Bible and read Romans 3:23-25.
8. Discuss:
   • What do these verses say about people? about God?
   • How does God take care of our sin?
9. With an adult's help, use the medicine dropper to add one drop of bleach to the water. Stir gently.

10. Add additional bleach, one drop at a time, until the water is clear.
11. Discuss:
    • How is adding bleach to colored water like adding Jesus to your life?
    • What can you do this week to let God add more Jesus to your life?
12. Read Matthew 5:8 on your handout through the glass of water one last time. Thank God that he wants to help you know him!

"GOD BLESSES THOSE WHOSE HEARTS ARE PURE, FOR THEY WILL SEE GOD" (Matthew 5:8).

KIDS' TRAVEL GUIDE TO THE BEATITUDES

Journey 10

God Blesses Those Who Work for Peace

Pathway Point: God calls us his children.

In-Focus Verse: "God blesses those who work for peace, for they will be called the children of God" (Matthew 5:9).

Travel Itinerary

In 1873, Horatio Spafford wrote a moving hymn that paints a verbal and musical picture of what peace is all about. In the good times and the bad times, a soul at peace will put trust in God and say, "It is well with my soul." What makes Spafford's hymn more powerful are the circumstances leading up to the penning of his iconic hymn.

Spafford was a lawyer in Chicago in the mid-1800's. A year after the death of his 4-year-old son, Spafford lost a huge amount of investment real estate to the Great Chicago Fire of 1871. A couple of years later, Spafford loaded his wife and four daughters on a ship headed to England. He was to join them soon after. En route, the ship collided with another ship and sank. His four daughters drowned, leaving his wife to send a note to Spafford stating, "Saved alone."

It's difficult to imagine the pain and despair Spafford must have felt upon receiving that note. Had he done something to offend God? First, his son dies at a young age; then a fire engulfs a huge investment; and now his daughters are gone. Spafford's world was turned upside-down.

History says that Spafford boarded a ship to join his wife. At the place where the ship his daughters and wife were on went down, Spafford penned the words that became the hymn so many of us are familiar with.

What makes a person write of "peace like a river" in the midst of mourning unspeakable tragedy?

When we think of peace, most of us think of it as absence of conflict or a state of well-being. In other words, when there's peace, then everything is right with the world. When things are going all wrong, there's no peace.

Scripture tells us something different about peace. It's the result of wholeness rather than an emotional state based on external factors. Perhaps author Scot McKnight defines it best: "Peace is when you've got what you need and need what you've got, when you love those you are with and are with the ones you love, and when you are doing good to others and they're doing good to you." This is the kind of peace we want children to strive for.

Jesus sought peace for his followers—peace of mind, peace of heart, and peace of being. His message was ultimately that of peace and hope. He is our greatest example of one who works for peace. He calls us to be at peace with God and with others. This means we become peacemakers, and we become different from the reigning culture. This is where this Beatitude has its real power: "God blesses those who work for peace, *for they will be called the children of God*" (Matthew 5:9). Peacemakers have a place in the kingdom of God.

DEPARTURE PRAYER

(up to 5 minutes)

In this prayer activity, children explore a world in need of peace and ask God to help them work for peace in their world.

Items to Pack:

Bible; newspapers and news magazines, or printed-out headlines (both positive and negative) from Internet news sources; several pairs of scissors; poster board; glue sticks; marker

Ask: • **Describe what you think a news headline is.**

• **If you had to think of a headline to describe your life right now, what would it be?**

Let each child have a chance to come up with a headline. If a child chooses to pass, that's fine.

Say: **News headlines can tell us a lot about what's happening in the world around us.**

Read four or five headlines, including good and bad news.

Ask: • **What do you think these headlines tell us about our world?**

Say: **A lot of things happen in our world. Some things are amazing and some things are sad. When Jesus was born, angels appeared to shepherds, and one of the things they said was, "Glory to God in highest heaven, and *peace* on earth to those with whom God is pleased" (Luke 2:14).**

TOUR GUIDE TIP Preview the headlines and advertisements in the news materials you use for this activity. Remove anything that isn't appropriate.

Peace on earth—that sounds great!

Ask: • **Based on the headlines we looked at, tell whether you think there's peace on earth today.**

• **What do you think peace on earth would look like?**

• **What, if anything, do you think Jesus' birth might have had to do with peace on earth?**

Say: **In some ways there's peace on earth. In other ways, there isn't. It can be hard to know what to do about situations—no matter how big or how small—where there's no peace. Let's read our verse for today: Matthew 5:9.**

Have a willing child read the verse, or read the verse yourself if you have younger kids.

Say: **In this verse, God calls us his children. As God's children, Jesus says *we* can work for peace. God wants us to be peacemakers in the world.**

Ask: • **What ideas do you have about what it means to be a peacemaker?**

Say: **Before we dive into what it means to be a peacemaker and how we can work for peace, we're going to pray. First, let's each cut out one headline that isn't so peaceful and glue it to the poster board.**

Write "Work for Peace" at the top of the poster board. Provide scissors and glue sticks for kids to each cut out a headline and glue it to the poster board.

Say: **As we talk to God, everyone place your hand on the headline you glued to the poster board, and quietly ask God how you can work for peace.**

Pray: **God, thank you for sending Jesus to bring peace to our world. There are times and places in our world that aren't peaceful. Please help us learn how to be peacemakers in the world around us. Please guide us to know where we can help, like in these headlines we posted here. In Jesus' name, amen.**

Say: **Let's put our "Work for Peace" poster aside for now. We'll come back to it later.**

Have kids help you gather the news stories, scissors, glue sticks, and poster board and set them aside. You'll be using them again for an activity at the end of the lesson.

(15 minutes)
Want/Need

Children discover that the first step to being a peacemaker is trusting God to take care of our needs.

Say: **Let's open the Bible and listen to Matthew 5:9 again: "God blesses those who work for peace, for they will be called the children of God."**

Say: **Before we know how to "work for peace" or be peacemakers, we have to know what peace is.**

Ask: • **Explain what you think peace is.** Allow time for discussion.

• **Why do you think we hope for peace in our world?**

You'll probably hear a variety of thoughts about whether or not there's peace on earth. Acknowledge each child's ideas; these are tough questions. Let kids' statements stand on their own. You're building rapport with kids, providing a safe environment to participate and explore what it means to be a peacemaker. Your reaction paves the way for kids to engage more deeply with the entire group as you progress through the lesson.

If you have a larger group, you can make more than one "Work for Peace" poster board.

Items to Pack:
Bible, small slips of paper, pencils or pens, bowl or hat

TOUR GUIDE TIP

Don't assume children know how to navigate the Bible. While they probably can use a computer, smartphone, or tablet to search for a verse, it's important to help them understand how the Bible is put together. Take a moment and show kids the book of Matthew in the Bible. Point out that the Bible is a book made up of many books and is separated into two large sections: the Old Testament, written before Jesus was born, and the New Testament, which is about Jesus' life and how the church began. Matthew is the first book in the New Testament.

FUN FACT

The Hebrew word for peace is *shalom*. In Bible times and today, Hebrew-speaking people greet and bid farewell to each other by saying "Shalom." It's like saying, "Peace be with you."

TOUR GUIDE TIP

If you have a smaller group, have kids write two or three things down on different slips of paper, and play more than one round of the game.

Say: **Those are all great ideas about peace. Now I want you to think of a time recently you felt peaceful or at peace.** (Be prepared with a personal example.) **One time I felt peaceful when…** (tell your story and explain what about that situation made your life peaceful).

Say: **Your turn. Turn to a partner. One of you will tell about a time you felt peaceful, and why. You'll have one minute; then on my signal, let your partner talk.**

Give partners time to share, giving a one-minute signal that it's the other person's turn to talk. Let kids talk for another minute; then gather kids' attention back to you. Invite any willing kids to share their experiences with the group.

Say: **Thanks for telling us about those peaceful times in your lives. From what we just talked about, peace can be a lot of different things.** Highlight some of the kids' examples.

Say: **One way to work for peace is to trust that God gives us what we need and to not worry so much. Here's what the Bible tells us about God taking care of us.**

Read aloud Matthew 6:31-33. Say: ◐ **God calls us his children. We can have peace because he gives us what we need.**

Ask: • **If God gives us everything we need, why do you think we still want more?**

• **Describe what kinds of things you worry about not having.**

• **Why do you think we worry about not having certain things?**

Say: **To find out more about this, let's play a little game called Want It, Need It.**

Give kids slips of paper and pens or pencils.

Say: **On the paper, write or draw one thing you think you need but don't have. Don't show anyone. When you're done, give me your paper.**

Collect the paper slips and pens or pencils. Place the slips in a bowl, hat, or other container from which they can be drawn.

Explain to kids that one half of your room is the Want It side, and the other half is the Need It side. Tell kids that you'll draw out the papers one by one and read what's on them. Kids will each vote on whether the thing is a want or a need by moving to the corresponding side of the room.

Say: **Remember: *Wants* are things we can survive without, and *needs* are things we can't survive without.**

Play the game until you've gone through all the slips of paper. If kids are fairly evenly divided on whether something is a want or a need, pause to let both

110

sides provide reasoning for why they voted the way they did. Tell kids they can change their minds at any time and change sides. After you've gone through all the paper slips, have kids sit down.

Ask: • **What surprised you about this game?**

• **Explain whether you changed your mind about whether something was a want or a need.**

• **How do you decide whether something is a want or a need in real life?**

• **Explain whether, right now, you already have everything you need.**

Say: **Most of us have what we need to survive—like food and people to love and take care of us. When we realize we have most of what we really need, we can feel at peace and become peacemakers because ⬤ God calls us his children and takes care of our needs.**

STORY EXCURSION

(10 minutes)
We're All in This Together

Children are faced with challenges they can only solve when they work for peace with each other.

Have kids look at the "Work for Peace" poster again.

Ask: • **What do you think all our headlines have in common, aside from not being peaceful?**

Let kids discuss their answers. Then say: **All these headlines involve people. If we were to investigate these stories, we'd probably find that part of the problem involves people not getting along. Being a peacemaker means we're peaceful with the people around us and we help other people have peace. Let's see what the Bible says about this.**

Read aloud Romans 12:16-18.

Ask: • **What do you think these verses say it takes to live in peace with others?**

Say: **Living in peace with others takes patience, kindness, forgiveness, and mercy. We're going to play a game called We're All in This Together to see what it means to "live in peace with everyone."**

For the game, choose one of the following.

Items to Pack:
Bible, "Work for Peace" poster from previous activity, long stick such as a broom handle (for the Levitating Stick activity), hula hoop toy (for the Hoop Pass activity)

TOUR GUIDE TIP

You can choose from three different activity options in this section, depending on your kids, space, and available resources.

Levitating Stick *(best for preteens)*

Form two equal groups. Have the groups line up shoulder-to-shoulder facing the other group with the lines only a few inches apart from each other. Have everyone hold their index finger, palm-side up, out in front of them. Once fingers are up, you'll be able to rest a single, long stick on everyone's index fingers in both lines. The challenge is for everyone to work together to lower the stick to the ground and then raise it back up. The catch is, everyone has to keep an index finger supporting the stick at all times. You'll quickly find that until everyone figures out how to work together, the stick will continue to rise or fall off everyone's fingers.

Hoop Pass *(best for elementary or mixed ages)*

Have kids form a circle holding hands. Then place a hula hoop toy between two kids so they clasp their hands through the hoop. The objective is to pass the hula hoop toy around the circle as quickly as possible—but kids can't let go of one another's hands at all. Do the challenge a couple of times to get faster each time. Kids will have to communicate and work together to succeed.

Untangled *(best for younger and mixed ages)*

Have kids form a circle. Have everyone reach across the circle and grab the hands of two different people, forming a tangled mess. The objective is to get untangled as quickly as possible without ever letting go of anyone's hands. (You may end up with more than one circle and with some kids facing in different directions. That's okay. The point is for *everyone* to get untangled.) Play a couple of times. Everyone will have to communicate and work together to get faster each time.

With each of these experiences, offer some guidance if kids get frustrated, but encourage them to work together to solve the challenge and succeed together. Once your group has completed the challenge, have kids form a circle. Read aloud Romans 12:16-18 again.

Ask: • **What was our challenge like for you?**

• **What happened when you didn't work well together?**

• **How did being peaceful with each other help you succeed?**

Say: **To be successful, you had to be peacemakers during the challenge. You had to work together and listen to each other's ideas.**

Ask: • **What was it like to have others listen to you?**

• **Why do you think you were able to complete the challenge?**

Say: **Being a peacemaker isn't always popular. Sometimes it's easier to take sides or worry about being right. Being a peacemaker can also be lonely when others take sides. But Jesus tells us that when we work for peace, we aren't alone because ⬤ God calls us his children.**

ADVENTURES IN GROWING

(10 minutes)

Known by Our Love

Kids look at the Bible to discover what it means to be called children of God.

Items to Pack:
Bibles; slips of paper with one of the following passages printed on each Matthew 22:34-40; 1 John 4:7-8; Luke 6:32-35; John 13:34-35

Have kids form groups of three or four. Give each group a Bible.

Say: **As peacemakers, we know that ⬤ God calls us his children. Sometimes we wonder what it means to be God's children.**

Ask: • **How can we find out what it means to be God's children?**

Say: **The Bible tells us exactly what it means to be a child of God. Each group is going to get a passage of Scripture to look up, in which is explained more about being children of God. Work with your group to find the Scripture and read it.**

Distribute a passage to each group. If you have more groups than passages, multiple groups can look up the same Scripture. Allow groups time to read their passage. Let older kids help younger kids. Then ask groups to discuss what their Scripture tells them about being God's children.

After two minutes, invite groups to tell everyone what they discovered.

Say: **Children of God will be known for how they love each other and how they love others. If peacemakers are called children of God, then that means peacemakers work for peace by loving each other and loving others.**

God made it easy for us to be a part of bringing peace to the world around us. If we make loving him and loving others our goal, then we'll be working for peace at the same time.

Items to Pack:

Bible, "Work for Peace" poster from previous activity, headlines from newspapers or news sources (from Departure Prayer activity), scissors, glue sticks, 1 copy per child of the "Adventures in Peacemaking" handout (at the end of this lesson), pens or pencils, Travel Journals

TOUR GUIDE TIP

If you have non-readers, have them brainstorm their own peaceful headlines. Cross out the negative ones and write new ones on the poster.

TOUR GUIDE TIP

When kids discuss practical ways they can live out what they're learning, they have more ownership of their faith. This also sparks further ideas, creativity, and connections with other children.

SOUVENIRS

(15 minutes)

Peacekeepers

Kids get to work together to come up with peacekeeping ideas they can put into practice.

Ask: • As God's children, how can we follow Jesus' message in Matthew 5:9?

• **What are ways we can be peacekeepers in real life?**

Say: **We get to be a part of bringing God's peace to the world. That sounds exciting!**

Have kids gather around the "Work for Peace" poster.

Say: **Look again at the headlines we cut out. There are a lot of people and places and situations without peace.**

For now, I want each of you to find another headline. This time, though, look for a headline that's about something good or peaceful and cut it out. We're going to replace these headlines with peaceful ones. Once you've found a new headline, cut it out and glue it on top of your negative headline.

Allow time for kids to work.

Say: **We've been talking a lot about being peacemakers. Now it's time to find real ways we can be peacemakers this week.**

Distribute pens or pencils and an "Adventures in Peacemaking" handout to each child.

Say: **Find a partner and talk about one way you can be at peace with what you already have. For example, rather than asking your mom or dad to buy you a new toy, you can pull out toys you haven't played with in a while and play with them. Write or draw what you and your partner come up with on the "Adventures in Peacemaking" handout.**

Allow children three minutes to talk with their partner and write down their ideas, and then invite willing kids to share ideas they came up with.

Say: **Those are great ways to be content and at peace with what God has given you.**

Now find a new partner. This time think about a specific person—maybe at home or school—you don't get along with very well. Talk about one thing you can do to get along with that person better this

week. Write or draw what you come up with on your "Adventures in Peacemaking" handout.

Allow children three minutes to talk with their new partner; then invite willing kids to talk about their ideas.

Say: **You all have great ideas to make peace with the people around you. Here's one more. Find another new partner, and this time talk about one way you can help bring peace to the world around you. This could be your neighborhood, school, state, or another country— anywhere. For example, you can get friends together and collect trash at a park. Don't forget to write or draw what you come up with on your "Adventures in Peacemaking" handout.**

Allow children three minutes to talk with their partner; then invite willing kids to talk about their ideas.

Distribute kids' Travel Journals and say: **You have great adventures in peacemaking ahead of you. You can take your "Adventures in Peacemaking" handout and add it to your Travel Journal as a reminder to follow through with your ideas.**

Collect the Travel Journals, and put them away till next week.

HOME AGAIN PRAYER	(up to 5 minutes)
	Kids pray for specific ways they can work for peace.

Have children stand in a circle for prayer.

Say: **As we end our journey today, remember that** **God calls us his children. God wants us to work for peace in the world around us.**

For the first part of our prayer, let's hold our hands open in front of us with our palms facing up, as a symbol of offering all our worries and needs to God.

Pray: **God, it's so easy for us to worry about things we don't have. Sometimes we forget that** **you call us your children, and you take care of our needs. Right now we ask you to help us trust you to take care of us. Please help us be content with what you've given us.**

Pause for a few seconds to allow children to quietly reflect.

Say: **Now let's hold hands as we pray and ask God to help us be at peace with the people around us.**

Pray: **God, it's so easy for us to take sides and worry about being right. There are a lot of times, God, that we want to get back at people**

During times like these, it's possible a child may bring up an abusive relationship. In such a situation, redirect the conversation and confidentially follow through with appropriate ministry procedures immediately following your gathering time.

Items to Pack:

who do wrong things to us. Help us to be different and work for peace with the people around us. And when it feels lonely to be a peacemaker, help us remember that you call us your children and we're part of your family.

Pause for a few seconds to allow children to quietly reflect.

Say: **Now let's turn around and face outward with our hands stretched out in front of us as we ask God to help us be peacemakers in the world around us.**

Pray: **God, there are broken parts of the world around us. There are people and places that don't have your peace. God, help us see how we can help bring your peace to the world around us. Give us courage to listen to you and do what you ask us to do in our world.**

In Jesus' name, amen.

Say: **As we finish today, let's leave with something called a benediction. A benediction is a prayer of blessing to encourage you as** 🌑 **God's children. This benediction comes from the Bible in Romans 15:33: "And now may God, who gives us his peace, be with you all. Amen."**

I can't wait to hear how God helps you work for peace this week!

ADVENTURES in PEACEMAKING

Write or draw what you discuss with your partner for each point below.

I can be at peace with what I have by...

I can be at peace with the people around me by...

I can work for peace in the world around me by...

God Blesses Those Who Are Punished for Doing Right

Pathway Point: ◕ God takes care of us.

In-Focus Verse: "God blesses those who are persecuted for doing right, for the Kingdom of Heaven is theirs" (Matthew 5:10).

Travel Itinerary

Jesus knew all too well that his followers would face tough times for their faith in him. So he wasn't only giving them insight about what lay ahead in Matthew 5:10, but he was also communicating that their struggles wouldn't be in vain. Jesus knew intimately how pain and persecution would go hand-in-hand with Christian faith; he went there long before we ever did. He encouraged his followers that day to stay focused on the kingdom of heaven—which was central to most of Jesus' teachings as he mentions it more than 30 times in the Gospel of Matthew alone.

At the root of Jesus' teaching was the idea that when persecution comes (as it inevitably does), we have an opportunity for our faith to grow and flourish. Kids have a strong sense of fairness and rightness, and they're acutely aware when that boundary is violated. They understand what it means to do right and play by the rules—and at the same time they're beginning to experience peer pressure and they've undoubtedly been on the wrong end of unfairness. Be extra sensitive to what types of persecution and pressure your kids face. Any type of persecution can be scary to face—whether you're a child or an adult—but with the reassurance that God never leaves us, we can have the courage to face it.

Soak in this lesson as an encouragement to you as much as the kids you minister to. Whatever you're facing this week, as you strive to do the right thing in your life and for your kids, may God continue to guide and care for you. And remember Jesus' promise: the kingdom of heaven will be yours!

Items to Pack: filled water balloons (1 for each group, plus a couple extra); an activity area outside or where the floor can get wet; several clean towels; upbeat Christian music; music player

DEPARTURE PRAYER (up to 5 minutes)

Through this prayer activity, kids discover that God can protect them.

Have kids form groups of about five and sit in circles. Say: **We're going to play Hot Potato, a game where you'll pass an item to someone next to you as quickly as possible as if it's too hot to hold.**

TOUR GUIDE TIP
If you have a smaller group, play as one group.

TOUR GUIDE TIP
Some children may need extra guidance as to how to gently pass a water balloon in the circle. If needed, have a volunteer on hand to help guide them during the game. Remind kids that the goal is to not have the balloon break—or end up holding it.

Items to Pack:
Bible, individually packed flowering bedding plants, foam cups, potting soil, 1 bucket or container and 1 scoop per group, spray bottles filled with water, markers, newspapers to cover your work area

Emphasize to kids to be extra careful with the water balloons, and let them know their group will only get one; if it breaks, they're out.

Say: **Here's how we'll play. Once the music starts, gently but quickly pass the water balloon to your left. When the music stops, whoever's holding the water balloon is out. Whatever you do, don't drop it!**

Distribute the balloons, one per group. Play until each group is down to one person. (Play more rounds if time allows.) If a group drops the balloon, have them sit on their hands until the game is over.

Say: **You all did great!**

Ask: • **What was this game like for you?**

• **Explain whether you were worried you might break the balloon and get wet.**

• **How did the skin of the balloon protect you from getting wet?**

Hold up a water balloon to demonstrate with.

Say: **A balloon's skin contains the water inside, even though it's thin and squishy. Unless you dropped it, the skin was strong enough to protect all of you from getting wet. Today we're going to learn more about how** **God takes care of us just like the balloon's skin protected us from getting wet.**

Pray: **God, thank you for being with us today and every day. Thank you for always taking care of us. Please help us remember that you protect and care for each of us just as these balloons protected us from getting wet. You are our great protector. In Jesus' name, amen.**

1st STOP DISCOVERY (15 minutes)
Flower Fun

Kids discover that just as God cares for flowers, he cares for them, too.

Have kids stay in their groups from earlier. Say: **Planting flowers is something a lot of people enjoy. They're beautiful, fun to care for, and rewarding to watch grow. I once...** (briefly share an appropriate experience regarding planting flowers or gardening and why you enjoyed it).

Spread out the newspapers so each group is sitting on them and has a workspace. Say: **I have flowers to share with you today. Let's pass around these flowers so you have a chance to touch and smell them.**

Pass around the individually packed flowers, sharing the names and different characteristics of the flowers if you can. Encourage kids to gently touch the flowers and smell their blooms.

Ask: • **What kinds of things do you notice about the flowers?**

• **Explain what you like about flowers. Why do you think they make people happy?**

Say: **Today we are going to plant flowers with our groups.** Have willing kids from each group gather ten scoops of dirt in a container, the scoop, plus one cup for each person in their group. Distribute two markers to each group. Then let kids each choose an individually packed flower to plant. Have all kids sit in their groups again.

Say: **Each of you will write your name on the front of a cup so you know which is yours.** Encourage older kids to help younger kids as needed.

Say: **You'll need to take turns to plant your flower. Your job is to care for each other today by helping and sharing within your group. When it's your turn, put two scoops of dirt into your cup so it's about two-thirds full. Then pass the scoop to the person next to you.** Allow time.

Now that you've filled your cups with dirt, take a finger and poke a hole in the middle of the dirt. Gently remove your flower from the container. Place your flower in the hole; then pack the dirt around the roots. If you'd like, you can spray your flower and dirt with the water.

Allow time, and then ask: • **Explain what you think a flower needs to grow.**

• **How do you think something as fragile as a flower can live and grow in our world?**

• **In what ways are we like or unlike these fragile flowers?**

Say: **God provides everything a flower needs, such as water and sunlight.**

Open your Bible and read aloud Luke 12:27-28a.

Ask: • **What do you think this verse says about how God cares for us?**

• **Why do you think God takes such good care of everything he created?**

• **What are ways God takes care of you?**

Say: **God created flowers to be beautiful and smell good, but also for many other important purposes. God also made sure the flowers would be cared for. If God ensures these flowers are taken care of, how much**

If you're short on time, have soil or dirt already in the cups. You can also put each group's items on a tray ahead of time; however, remember that part of this experience is to have kids help one another, so emphasize that aspect of the project.

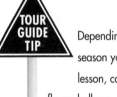

Depending on the season you do this lesson, consider having flower bulbs or seeds for kids to plant rather than the actual flower. Still provide full-grown flowers for the kids to look at, smell, and touch.

FUN FACT All 50 states have a state flower, and most countries around the world have a national flower. The national flower of the United States is the rose.

more will he make sure you're taken care of? **God cares for you.**

At the end of our lesson, you can take these flowers home. Then every time you look at or smell your flower, remember that **God takes care of you.**

Items to Pack:

Bible, 2 cardboard "shields" (2x2-foot cardboard squares), lots of paper balls, masking tape, timer or stopwatch, mini candy bars

ALLERGY ALERT ▶ Check with parents about allergies and dietary concerns, and post a copy of the "Allergy Alert" sign (at the end of this book) where parents will see it.

TOUR GUIDE TIP

If you have uneven numbers, join in so everyone has a partner.

STORY EXCURSION

(10 minutes)

Right Way

Kids explore why it's important to do what's right.

Say: **When Jesus sat on the hillside and talked to the huge crowd, he had some important things to say. The Beatitude we're focused on today is a really important one because it's something most of us can relate to. Jesus said, "God blesses those who are persecuted for doing right, for the Kingdom of Heaven is theirs."**

Ask: • **What do you think Jesus meant when he said this?**

• **Tell about a time you did the right thing but got into trouble for it.** (Be prepared to share an appropriate example from your own life.)

• **What was that experience like for you?**

Say: **It can be really hard when you do the right thing and get in trouble for it. That doesn't really seem fair. But in Jesus' life, he experienced a lot of unfairness when he did the right thing, and he knew his followers would, too. Still, he encourages us to keep standing up for what's right because even though we may be persecuted for it,** **God will take care of us. Let's explore what it's like to do the right thing.**

Have kids form pairs.

Say: **Look at your partner. One of you will be Jessie, who does the right thing. Your partner, Charlie, doesn't do the right thing. Take a moment to decide who's who.**

Allow time. If these names don't work for your group, change them to other gender-neutral names. While kids decide, spread out the candy bars on a table or counter where all the kids can see.

Say: **Ready? Here's your scenario. You, your partner, and some other friends have walked into a grocery store and down the candy aisle. Charlie wants to steal a candy bar. Jessie doesn't. You'll have two minutes to act this out with your partner, with each of you trying to convince the other to agree with your perspective to steal or not to steal. Ready, go!**

KIDS' TRAVEL GUIDE TO THE BEATITUDES

Let the action begin, but about 15 seconds in, say: **Oh wait, I need to check on something. Continue trying to convince your partner while I'm gone—but don't touch these yummy candy bars.**

Allow two minutes for kids to role-play. Leave the area, but stay somewhere close and out of sight where you can monitor what happens.

When you re-enter the room, say: **Great job! Give yourselves a round of applause.** Have kids sit in a circle.

Ask: • **Explain what you were thinking and saying if you played Charlie in this scenario, or if you played Jessie.**

• **When in real life have you been in a situation like this?**

• **Explain whether it's hard to do the right thing when others want you to do the wrong thing.**

• **What was it like for you when I left you with all these candy bars?**

• **Explain why you did or didn't take a candy bar while I was away.**

Say: **Doing right can be difficult sometimes. Sometimes we have to do the right thing even when it doesn't feel good. Sometimes we have to do the right thing even when others don't want us to. Jesus faced those things too, and he understands what it's like. That's why he spoke to people who he knew would be persecuted for doing right, and he wanted us to feel comforted knowing 🌐 God takes care of us.**

Let kids take a candy treat and eat it. Open your Bible and read aloud Matthew 5:10.

Say: ***Persecuted* is a big word, and it basically means to be mistreated. Jesus says in heaven, God will reward people who are mistreated for doing the right thing. He knows it can be hard to do what's right, especially if people disagree with you. But God blesses us when we stand strong for what's right. He blesses us because 🌐 God cares about us. Let's learn more about this by playing a game.**

Place a masking-tape line down the center of your activity area, and mark each of the areas using the following diagram. Ask for three willing kids to take these roles: One will be the Walker and will walk the center line during the game, and the other two will be Shielders and will hold the cardboard shields to fend off a paper-ball assault.

With the rest of the kids, form two teams and have each team go to a different side of the room. Place a pile of paper balls in front of each team. Teams will face each other with the line between the two groups. Get everyone in position before explaining the rules. (See the diagram for the layout.)

FUN FACT

In 1847, Fry's chocolate factory in England molded the first-ever chocolate bar suitable for widespread consumption.

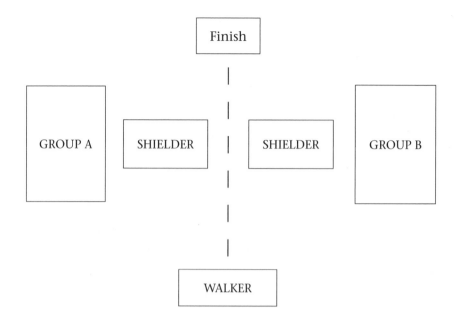

Say: **This game is called Walk the Line. The Walker will walk the line to the finish area, while others try to knock the Walker off course with paper balls. Both teams have their own paper balls on opposite sides of the line. Your goal is to try to tag the Walker with a paper ball. Shielders hold the cardboard shields and will try to protect the Walker, but they must stand at the middle of the line until the Walker reaches them. Walker, when I say "Go!" walk along the line while trying to dodge the paper balls. When you make it to the middle of the line where the Shielders are, they can escort you the rest of the way with their cardboard shields protecting you.**

Walk through the game once so kids all know their roles.

Say: **Ready, go!**

Play a few times, trading roles. Ask: • **What was this game like for you?**

• **What was it like for you to have people pelting you with paper balls?**

• **How did the Shielders help stop the attack?**

• **How is this game like or unlike what it's like in real life to be pelted for doing the right thing?**

Say: **Great job! Our Walkers got help when they made it halfway through. When we do what's right, God is still with us and ⬙ will take care of us. Let's clean up and enjoy a snack.**

Ask kids to help clean up.

ADVENTURES IN GROWING

(10 minutes)

Food for Thought

Serve children each two chocolate chip cookies on napkins with small cups of milk, but have them wait to eat.

Say: **Chocolate chip cookies are known as a "comfort" snack, something a lot of people like to eat when they're feeling down or just want something yummy. As you eat, think about how God cares for us and protects us. My challenge to you is to protect the chocolate chips in your cookie by eating around them. Ready, go!**

As children nibble, ask: • **Tell about a time God took care of you.**

• **Why do you think it matters to God that we do the right thing?**

• **What's one way you can stand up for what's right this week?**

Say: **God wants us to do what's right even if we're the only ones. And he wants us to remember that he'll help us through it. Doing what's right makes a difference. When we follow God, doing what's right is a part of our responsibility to him. Just as we've talked about today, if we do what's right and people persecute us for it, God still blesses us.**

Encourage kids to eat all the rest of their cookies; then have them help you clean up.

SOUVENIRS →

(10 minutes)

God Cares Chart

Kids think through how God truly cares about them every day.

Distribute kids' Travel Journals. Ensure each child has a handout, crayons, and a pencil.

Ask: • **Explain how you know if someone cares about you.**

• **Describe ways people show they care about each other.**

• **Tell us about someone you care about.**

Say: **Those are great examples. We're going to explore ways we can see that 🌐 God takes cares of us in everyday life.**

On your "Places I Go, People I Know" handout, there are six boxes. In each box, write or draw a way that God takes cares of you at that place or with those people. How does God take care of you at

Items to Pack:

chocolate chip cookies, milk, napkins, small cups
ALLERGY ALERT ▸ Check with parents about allergies and dietary concerns, and post a copy of the "Allergy Alert" sign (at the end of this book) where parents will see it.

Items to Pack:

1 copy per child of the "Places I Go, People I Know" handout (at the end of this lesson), crayons, pencils, Travel Journals

your home, school, and church? How does God take care of you with your family, friends, and by yourself? Take time to think of examples of how God has taken care of you at each place and with each person.

For me, one way God has taken care is... (tell kids an appropriate example of how God has taken care of you at a place and with other people).

Say: **Sometimes it's easy to see how God takes care of us, like how he provides food to eat or air to breathe. Other times we have to really look hard to see how God takes care of us, like how a prayer we thought he ignored ended up protecting us. God cares for us in big and small ways. Each day let's focus on how God takes care of us and how he wants us to stand up for what's right.**

Have kids add their handouts to their Travel Journals. Collect them, and put them away till next week.

HOME AGAIN PRAYER

(5 minutes)

Have kids form a circle.

Say: **Now link arms with the people next to you to make a chain. Today we learned that God takes care of us and he wants us to do what's right every day no matter what. With our linked arms we represent a chain, which is hard to break. So are God's promises and blessings. As we remain linked, let's pray for the person on our right. If you don't know that person's name, go ahead and ask it now.**

Allow time.

Say: **When it's your turn, you'll pray, "God, please take care of** [child's name on their right] **this week as he or she does what's right." I'll begin and we'll go around the circle to the right. I'll end the prayer. Let's pray.**

Pray: **God, please take care of** [child on your right] **this week as he or she does what's right.**

Give kids time to pray for each other, and help any who need extra prompting.

Pray: **Thank you, God, for teaching us what it means to do what's right. Thank you for reminding us that you care so much about us, even more than the flowers you provide for. As we leave, please help all of us do what's right this week, no matter what. God, thank** you for continuing to take care of us each day. Please help us see how you take care of us. In Jesus' name, amen.

Say: **Thank you for praying with me; all of you did a great job. As you leave here today, remember to take your flowers home with you. You can plant them outside or you can take care of them in your home. Each time you see your flower or smell it, remember that** 🌐 **God takes care of you. Be on the lookout this week to see God taking care of you, and come next week ready to tell about it.**

Places I Go, People I Know

Directions: Write or draw an example of how God takes cares of you at that place or with those people.

How does God take care of you when you're:

1. AT HOME

2. AT SCHOOL

3. AT CHURCH

4. WITH YOUR FAMILY

5. WITH YOUR FRIENDS

6. BY YOURSELF

KIDS' TRAVEL GUIDE TO THE BEATITUDES

JOURNEY

12 God Blesses Those Who Are Made Fun Of

Pathway Point: ● God says we belong to him.

In-Focus Verse: "God blesses you when people mock you and persecute you and lie about you and say all sorts of evil things against you because you are my followers" (Matthew 5:11).

Travel Itinerary

This particular Beatitude comes with a long list of reasons we can impress it upon our kids in this age of bullying and aggression. Bullying has become a staple of childhood it seems, and it starts at younger and younger ages. If ever there were an expert on how to handle being mocked and mistreated, it's Jesus. He experienced the worst of scorn and abuse from crowds leading up to his crucifixion and death, and yet he asked God to forgive his tormentors. He knew, despite his pain and humiliation, that God would bless him. Even in his deepest distress, he cried out to God. And, following his death, God did bless him, giving him his rightful due in heaven.

If ever there were a model for how to handle and persevere through being mocked, mistreated, and scorned, it's Jesus. And his example and message is vitally important for your kids to imprint upon their hearts. They'll face hurtful challenges that may make them doubt themselves and wonder whether they have value. When you teach this lesson with prayerful consideration, approach the topic of bullying with sensitivity and understanding. All kids can relate to what this feels like, and quite frankly, this may be their strongest connection to seeing Jesus as a real man who suffered, too. Remind kids that your group is a safe, caring environment where they can feel comfortable sharing their thoughts. And if you find children are facing bullying at their school or even at home, encourage them to find a safe adult to talk with about it, someone who'll help guide them through it. Most of all, encourage them to lean on Jesus and remember his words: "God blesses you when people mock you and persecute you and lie about you and say all sorts of evil things against you." Give kids hope by letting them know that no matter what, they don't face those feelings alone.

Items to Pack:
4 pairs of adult-size shoes

TOUR GUIDE TIP

Younger kids may need extra help knowing which foot to put their borrowed shoes on or with tying laces. This is a great opportunity to have some older kids help younger ones.

TOUR GUIDE TIP

Monitor this activity closely so kids don't attempt to force on their borrowed shoes if they don't fit. Emphasize that kids with smaller shoes should only put their toes into the shoes.

FUN FACT

It's likely that Jesus walked around in thin sandals or with bare feet. Still today there are tribes around the world where people don't wear shoes, but instead walk or run with bare feet.

DEPARTURE PRAYER

(10 minutes)

During this prayer kids experience what it feels like to not belong.

Say: **Please take off both your shoes and put them in a big pile by me. I'm even taking off my shoes, too. Once you've added your shoes to the pile, you can sit down.**

Allow time. Add your shoes to the pile as well as the adult-size shoes.

Say: **In a moment, you'll have 30 seconds to find a pair of shoes that doesn't belong to you and try to put them on. Remember—they can't be your own shoes. If they're small, that's okay, but don't force them to fit, just put your toes in. We don't want any broken shoes today. Ready, go!**

Give kids about 30 seconds to find a different pair of shoes. Look for the smallest pair of shoes and put them only on your toes.

Say: **It looks like everyone found a pair of shoes. The ones I found are pretty small; they don't fit quite right. Some of you have shoes that are too big, and some have ones that are too small.**

Ask: • **Describe what it feels like to be wearing these shoes that don't belong to you.**

• **What would you think if I told you to wear these shoes the rest of the day?**

• **How is this like or unlike when we feel out of place or like we don't belong?**

Say: **Trying to fit into someone else's shoes is a lot like how it feels to try to fit in when we feel we don't belong. Jesus knew a lot about what that feels like. Before he died, some people were very mean to him. They mocked him and made fun of him. So today we're going to explore 🌓 what it means to belong to God, especially when other people are mean or do things to hurt you.**

Give kids time to find and put on their own shoes; then ask them to sit.

Say: **It should feel a lot better to have on your own shoes now. We all feel more comfortable in our own shoes, and probably pretty uncomfortable in someone else's shoes. Let's keep this in mind as we open in prayer.**

Pray: **God, thank you for our time together today. We know you know what it feels like to not belong, and we ask that you be with us every time we feel like we don't belong—just like how it felt when we** had on someone else's shoes. Please be with us each time we feel out of place or mocked. Thank you for all the times we feel like we do belong—like here at church with our friends. Please help us remember we belong to you. In Jesus' name, amen.

1st STOP DISCOVERY

(15 minutes)

Puzzle Time

Kids discover that they belong to God.

Say: **Puzzles are meant to be challenging and fun. I remember a time when...** (tell about a good memory you have of putting puzzles together or what you like about them).

Distribute a piece of the puzzle to each child. Place the black pens or markers in easy reach. Take a puzzle piece for yourself and have any other adult volunteers do the same. Do not show kids the "big picture" or what the completed puzzle would look like.

Say: **When you get a puzzle piece, write your name on the back.** (Have older kids help younger ones if they need it.) **Then pass along the pen or marker but hold onto your puzzle piece.**

Allow time. Then ask: • **Explain what the result is when you put a puzzle completely together.**

• **What happens if pieces of the puzzle are missing?**

• **Take a close look at your puzzle piece. Explain what you think the completed puzzle will look like.**

Say: **Each puzzle piece is a small piece of the big picture. Without all the pieces in the right spots, we can't see the "big picture." We put puzzles together to see the big picture. Each piece only gives us a small glimpse of the whole, and it doesn't make a lot of sense. Let's put our puzzle together so we can see what it looks like.**

Encourage kids to work together to put the puzzle together, but have them do it using the back of the puzzle where their names are written facing up. If you have extra pieces, include them so the puzzle will be complete. And don't forget your piece and any other adults' pieces, as well.

Say: **You did a great job finishing this puzzle. We'll come back to it in a moment, but first please sit down.**

Read 1 Corinthians 3:23: **"And you belong to Christ, and Christ belongs to God."**

Items to Pack:
Bible, simple puzzle with enough pieces for each child in your group or slightly more, black pens or markers

FUN FACT

The first jigsaw puzzle was produced around 1760 by John Spilsbury of London. Puzzles were originally called "dissections"—a little less fun than the "jigsaw puzzle" they came to be known as in 1880.

TOUR GUIDE TIP

If you have fewer kids than puzzle pieces, include the pieces without a name in the puzzle and remind kids that those pieces represent friends or family who haven't come to church yet—because there's always room to add more people into God's big picture.

TOUR GUIDE TIP

To make completing the puzzle quicker and easier, start with border (or straight-edged) pieces-. Once the frame is complete, move into the inside of the puzzle.

Items to Pack:

Bible

Ask: • **What was it like to put together the puzzle upside-down?**

• **What do you think it means to "belong" to something or someone?**

• **Why do you think God wants us to belong to him?**

Say: **Belonging to something means to be part of it. Kind of like the shoes on your feet belong to you—they're your property and part of what you're wearing today. Let's listen to that Scripture again: "And you belong to Christ, and Christ belongs to God."**

This Scripture is saying that if we follow Jesus,  we belong to him. Everyone who is friends with Jesus is on his team.

It doesn't matter what we look like, how we dress, where we live, what sport we play or don't play, who our family is, what our grades are—none of that matters. If you love Jesus, then you belong to Jesus. He said in this Beatitude that we are his. God created you to be the unique person you are, and he loves you.

Let's take another look at our puzzle.

Ask: • **What do you see when you look at this completed puzzle?**

• **How is this finished puzzle with our names like or unlike what it means to belong to God?**

Say: **It doesn't have a big pretty picture that we can all see—but it does have the big picture of all our names connected together. Just as Jesus said, we all belong to God. This puzzle shows that we're all connected. Each piece belongs to the entire puzzle, just as each of us belongs to God and is a part of his big-picture plan.**

STORY EXCURSION

(up to 10 minutes)

Sticks and Stones

Kids explore why they belong to God and what that means.

Say: **Let's play a game of Follow the Leader where we all follow one person's lead.**

Have kids stand in a line behind you, and tell them to follow you around the room. Remind kids to follow you wherever you go, even if an obstacle comes up.

Make the game fun as you twist and turn or climb over or under things. To increase the challenge, ask older kids or volunteers to assist by inserting obstacles—after you've already passed by—for kids to maneuver behind you. Ideas for obstacles could include putting chairs in the path, standing in kids' way, or using a table to block the path so kids have to crawl under. Ensure the path is a little difficult to follow—but not too difficult. After a winding path, lead kids back to their seats.

Say: **Thank you for following me wherever I went, despite lots of obstacles.**

Ask: • **What was this game like for you?**

• **Explain what it's like to follow someone—like a parent or friend—in real life.**

• **Why do we follow people?**

Say: **One of the most important people we can follow is Jesus.** Read Matthew 5:11: "**God blesses you when people mock you and persecute you and lie about you and say all sorts of evil things against you because you are my followers.**"

Ask: • **What do you think this Beatitude means?**

• **Why do you think it matters to Jesus if you are mocked, lied about, or persecuted?**

• **What do you think knowing that Jesus says you belong to him?**

Say: **People have been mocked by others for a long time—all the way back to before Jesus' time. Jesus himself knows what it's like to be mocked; people were cruel and mocked him as he was carrying the cross to his crucifixion. That's why we can trust what Jesus says: If people make fun of you or lie about you because you follow me, God will bless you.**

Some of you may have a hard time being teased at school or maybe even in other places, and that can hurt. But what we're learning today is that no matter what people say about you, no matter what they call you or tell others about you, nothing changes the truth. The truth is that God created you and when you follow him, 🌀 you belong to God.

🛑 **ADVENTURES IN GROWING**

(up to 15 minutes)
Food for Thought

Hold up a cluster of grapes.

Say: **For a grape to grow, it must be attached to a cluster of grapes. For that cluster to grow, it must be attached to a grapevine. If the grape is separated from its cluster or if the cluster is separated from its vine, it won't grow anymore. As**

Items to Pack:
seedless grapes cut into small bunches, water, cups, napkins, whiteboard, dry-erase markers
ALLERGY ALERT ▶ Check with parents about allergies and dietary concerns, and post a copy of the "Allergy Alert" sign (at the end of this book) where parents will see it.

you enjoy your grapes, remember that 🜨 just as these grapes belong to their vine, you belong to God.

Distribute the grapes, along with napkins an cups of water. As children enjoy their snack, ask: • **Why do you think it matters to Jesus when we're mocked or lied about?**

Say: **Being bullied, mocked, or teased hurts. But God says he'll bless you as you experience that.**

Ask: • **How have you seen or experienced bullying?**

• **What could you say to a bully that might stop his or her actions?**

• **How do you think God wants us to handle a bully?**

These questions may spark sensitive discussion from some of your kids, so allow plenty of time and give kids guidance if they need it.

Ask: • **What do you think it means to follow God?**

• **What are ways we can follow God in our daily lives?**

• **How do you think God can help us as we deal with bullies?**

Say: **We can follow God in our daily lives by spending time with him, by reading our Bibles or by praying, and also by being obedient to what he asks us to do, such as being nice to other people.**

Have kids help you clean up the snack.

Say: **For some schools and people, bullying is a serious problem. If we do our part to obey God and remember that 🜨 we belong to him, we can help make a difference. When we remember that other people around us belong to God, too, we'll remember to treat them better and to stand up for them when they're being mocked. You belong to God; he created you and made you special. But he also created your neighbors, friends, and even bullies at school.**

Ask: • **Keeping that in mind, what are ways we can treat others around us better?**

Encourage kids to come up with at least 10 ideas they could do to be kinder to others, and write them on the whiteboard. Some starter ideas could include encouraging people, sticking up for someone, or helping people when they're sad or hurt.

Say: **These are great ideas. Most of these you could do this very week. Take a look at our list, and choose at least one or two things to do this week to be nicer to people around you.**

Allow time. Encourage older kids to read through the list with kids who can't read yet.

Say: **I challenge each of you, myself included, to do at least one nice thing for someone else this week. Next week we'll report back on what we did. I can't wait to hear your stories.**

SOUVENIRS →

(up to 10 minutes)

Encouragement Chain

Kids have an opportunity to encourage each other through their words.

Say: **One thing that can be on our list is to encourage people. Today let's get started early and do that for someone else in our group.**

Have kids form a circle on the floor. Then ask for a willing child to help distribute strips of paper and pens or pencils.

Say: **On your strip of paper, write a compliment or something nice about the person sitting on your right. Once you've finished, bring your paper up front so we can staple it into a chain.**

Allow time. While kids work, write one compliment for the adults who are assisting you, or for your group as a whole. As the kids bring up their paper strips, have someone staple the first one into a circle, with the writing facing out. For each additional paper, thread it through the previous circle and staple it, always with the writing facing out. Once the chain is complete, spread it out so kids can see how big it is.

Have kids gather around the chain.

Say: **Look how big your encouragement chain is! Let's all grab hold of this chain as I read each encouraging word.**

Have everyone take hold of the chain as you read each comment aloud.

Say: **Keep holding our chain of encouragement. Now close your eyes, and I'll pray for each of you.**

Pray: **Dear God, thank you for the encouraging words we've shared. Please speak these encouraging words straight to our hearts today. Remind each of us of how special we are to each other and to you. God, help us to know that these encouraging words are true and that ⬤ we belong to you. In Jesus' name, amen.**

Say: **Let's find a place to hang up this encouragement chain as a reminder that one encouraging word can have a big result and make a difference for someone who's feeling sad or left out.**

Items to Pack:
1 strip of paper per child from the "Encouragement Chain" handout (at the end of this lesson), pencils or pens, stapler

TOUR GUIDE TIP
For younger kids, writing encouragements may be difficult. If possible, have an adult or older child help younger ones write their compliment on their paper strip.

FUN FACT
Paper chains are a widespread tradition often associated with counting down to holidays, special events, or other special days.

TOUR GUIDE TIP
If you have a smaller group, let kids wrap themselves in the encouragement chain, and pray for each child individually.

TOUR GUIDE TIP

If you have younger children, have kids tear up their papers rather than using a paper shredder. Once they've torn up their paper and thrown it away, give them their handout.

TOUR GUIDE TIP

When using a paper shredder, use extreme caution and safety. Keep it out of kids' reach. When not in use, turn it off and unplug it. Have an adult volunteer monitor the shredder the entire time it's turned on. Have the adult help kids shred their paper, ensuring kids keep their hands at least 12 inches from the shredder.

HOME AGAIN PRAYER (up to 5 minutes)

Distribute blank pieces of paper and pens or pencils.

Say: **Take a few minutes to think about a time someone made fun of you. Then write or draw how that made you feel. Feel free to move away by yourself for this activity. When you're done, you can come up and, with an adult's help, shred your paper. Keep your hands away from the shredder; let the adult push the paper through it. As your paper shreds, remember what we learned today: When you follow God and people make fun of you, he will bless you. As you watch that paper shred, please take a moment to pray silently to God and thank him that you belong to him.**

Give kids time to write or draw on their papers. Encourage them to come up and have their paper shredded. As they walk away, give kids each a copy of the "I Belong to God" handout. Once everyone has finished shredding and praying, gather their attention back to you.

Say: **The new paper is something you'll keep to remind you that you belong to God. We'll keep it in your Travel Journal, and it'll be a reminder of what we learned today. Let's take a look.**

Read the handout.

Say: **Each of you belongs to God. "Thank you for making me so wonderfully complex! Your workmanship is marvelous—how well I know it"—Psalm 139:14.**

Have kids write their names in the blank on their pages.

Let's close in prayer. While I pray, you can doodle on your handout, kind of like drawing your own prayer to God.

Pray: **God, thank you for each child here today. Thank you that we belong to you. Please protect each of these kids at school, at home, and wherever they go. Remind them always that they belong to you. Help them to be kind to others, and when others are mean, bless them because of it. In Jesus' name, amen.**

Have kids place their papers in their Travel Journals, and then collect them and put them away till next week.

Say: **As we leave today, remember that each of you is special, created by God. You belong to him. If bullying is something you're struggling with, find an adult you can talk to about it, whether it's me, another volunteer, your teacher, or especially your parent. This** week wherever you go, remember to be kind and nice to each person you meet. I can't wait to hear next week what you did to be kind or to encourage someone else.

Encouragement Chain

Directions: Cut along the dotted lines and give each child one strip of paper. Have kids write on the paper a compliment or something nice about someone in your group. Then staple the links together to form one large chain.

_____

belongs to God.

"Thank you for making me so wonderfully complex!
Your workmanship is marvelous—how well I know it."

PSALM 139:14

A Great Reward Awaits

Pathway Point:  God wants us to live for him.

In-Focus Verse: "Be happy about it! Be very glad! For a great reward awaits you in heaven. And remember, the ancient prophets were persecuted in the same way" (Matthew 5:12).

Travel Itinerary

There are many reasons the Beatitudes are some of the most beloved and quoted teachings of Jesus' ministry. They bring comfort, solace, insight, and encouragement. Jesus was careful to give a detailed path we could follow to gain the rewards of heaven and find peace in this challenging earthly life. He made it clear that attitude is everything. Our lives as his followers won't be easy and our faith won't always be received well by others. We'll face persecution, mockery, and cruelty. He knew all this and was preparing all his followers for it—because he knew the rewards of our faith would be immeasurable.

Matthew 5:12 is a final encouragement that tells us we can approach trials, challenges, and hardship with an attitude of humility, joy, and hope—because our reward in heaven will far outweigh our earthly suffering. In this life we will endure; in heaven we will celebrate, with no more tears, no more trials.

Your kids will find a challenge in this final lesson to set their sights on God and hold tight to him whenever trials come. Whatever they're facing this week, this month, or later in life—they can have faith in Jesus' words that their faith and faithfulness will be rewarded. Use this lesson to motivate kids to live for God through their words and actions, while remembering that their love for Jesus will always shine for others to see.

DEPARTURE PRAYER | _(10 minutes)_
In this playful prayer, children discover that God wants us to live for him.

Hide the gems around your room before kids arrive. Hide four gems per child.

While kids arrive, set out the board games ready to play around the room. Encourage kids to play for several minutes after your session begins. Call time after about five minutes.

Items to Pack:
several simple, age-appropriate board games (1 game per 4 kids); 4 adhesive-backed gems per child; 1 copy of the "Crown Template" (at the end of this lesson)

TOUR GUIDE TIP

You'll later reveal the paper as a crown (and you don't want kids to know this yet), so place the paper with the crown outline face-down as the location for kids to bring their found gems.

FUN FACT

While digging in Egyptian tombs, archaeologists found games carved from stone and marble that were around in Jesus' day. Backgammon was among the ancient games found.

Biblical scholars who study children's activities during Bible times have found that Jewish children played with carved wooden lions and crocodiles with movable parts; rattles; dolls; hoops; and clay discuses.

Have kids leave the games where they are and sit in a circle.

Say: **I hope you enjoyed the games.**

Ask: • **Describe what was going on in the game when I told you it was time to stop.**

• **Why do you think people like to play games?**

• **Aside from winning, tell what other things you like about playing games.**

Say: **Most people love to play games because they make us laugh and we have a good time. And we like to be in on the action. It can be fun to watch friends play a game, but if you don't play, you can't win or get the reward of having a good time.**

Just like you got in on the action playing these games, God wants us to get in on the action of living for him.

Hold up a gem and the blank side of the crown template, making sure you only show kids the side of the paper without the crown. Say: **Let's play another game. You'll have two minutes to find all the hidden gems around the room. As you find a gem, come and set it on this paper, and then go search for more until you've each found four. On "go," start searching! Ready, go!**

When time is up, have kids sit in a circle around the gems on the paper. Say: **We're going to learn more today about what it means to live for God. Let's start by asking God to be with us today.**

As I pray, look closely at the gems on the paper. Listen carefully because you're going to touch your eyes, ears, and mouth as I pray.

Pray: **God, just like we actively played games and searched for the gems, we want to discover how to get in on the action of living for you. Please be with us as we learn about the rewards that await us in heaven and how we can find joy in everyday life here on earth, even when it's hard.**

Instruct kids to touch each body part you mention in the following part of your prayer. Say: **God, help us use our eyes to see what you want us to see.**

Help us use our mouths to say what you want us to say.

Help us use our ears to hear what you want us to hear as we learn how to live for you. Thank you, God. In Jesus' name, amen.

Set aside the crown template and gems.

1st STOP DISCOVERY

(20 minutes)

Leap for Joy

Kids play a game to discover that Jesus wants us to follow him to inherit the rewards—even when it's challenging.

Items to Pack:

masking tape

Say: **There are times when living for God is fun and exciting, like playing a fun game. But sometimes it's hard and even frustrating when we face tough problems or people who mistreat us. We have the Bible to help us through those times. With the Bible, we can get in on the action of life and still know how to handle problems that come up while we're living for God.**

Ask: • **Why do you think it can sometimes be difficult or challenging to live for God?**

Depending on the size and age of your group, place a 10-inch masking-tape starting line at one end of your room for each group of five kids. For each starting line, place a masking-tape X on the floor 6 inches from that line. Place another X 12 inches from the previous X, and the next X at 24 inches from the previous one. Adjust these distances as needed for your age group.

Explain to kids that they'll take turns leaping from marks on the floor that are more difficult with each leap. Kids who aren't leaping will cheer on the leapers. Let all kids who want to participate do so.

Have kids line up behind a start line and play for about five minutes. Ensure that every child who wants to leap has the opportunity. As kids leap, encourage the others to cheer.

Afterward, have kids sit in a circle. Say: **Great leaping! Great cheering!**

Ask: • **Explain whether you think you were successful at leaping.**

• **Describe what it was like to hear your friends cheer for you. What was it like to cheer on a friend who was leaping?**

• **What are ways we cheer for each other in real life to help our friends live for God and stay focused on him?**

• **Why do you think it's important to encourage each other to stay focused on God, even when other things make it hard?**

Say: **Cheering each other on is a great way to help each other to not quit and to do our best. Turn to a partner and think of two ways you can encourage each other to live for God. Think of things you can say and do.**

Allow time.

TOUR GUIDE TIP

Emphasize to kids that living for God isn't all about rules—it's about having a relationship with him. God gave us commandments to live by, but he also knows we fall short. That's why he offers us grace and forgiveness for our sins. He wants to be our friend and a daily presence in our lives!

TOUR GUIDE TIP

If you have kids who aren't able to jump, simply substitute leaping with tossing a beanbag and trying to land it on the X marks.

Say: **Just like we cheered each other on, we can support each other to stay focused on God.** 🌑 **God wants us to live for him.**

(10 minutes)

The Crown

Children learn that God rewards us when we live for him.

Say: **We've been talking about how** 🌑 **God wants us to live for him. Let's talk about the rewards of living for God.**

Read aloud Matthew 5:12.

Say: **The ancient prophets who told people about God were persecuted, or mistreated, for believing in him. People talked bad about them, left them out, and even hurt them just because they lived for God. Yet the Bible encouraged them—and us—to be** *happy* **when we're mistreated.**

Ask: • **Why do you think Jesus told people to be happy when others mistreated them?**

• **Explain whether you think our reward in heaven is worth having other people mistreat us for believing in Jesus.**

• **Why do you think it's important to remain happy, no matter the situation?**

Say: **Throughout the Bible, there are examples of others who lived for God and who were rewarded for their faith. Let's find out more.**

The Bible tells us that God gives crowns to people who live for him. Let's learn about five crowns by looking at Bible passages.

Distribute copies of the "Five Crowns" handout and a pencil to each child.

Have kids form five groups. (Ensure that groups have mixed ages if you have more than one age level in your class.) Give each group a Bible. Say: **You'll work with your group to discover what's behind these important crowns. I'll give each group a passage to research. Your job is to label the crown with ideas about someone who might wear that crown. For instance, if you read the person would need to teach others about God, one label could be "teacher."**

You may want to know what the "official" names of the crowns are. Don't expect kids to title them with these words—they'll come up with great observations on their own. Don't correct kids' titles; just let them know what the scholars called them.

Items to Pack:

Bibles, the gem-covered paper from the opening prayer experience, scissors, 1 copy per child of the "Five Crowns" handout (at the end of this lesson), pencils, Travel Journals

---

FUN FACT

The concept of the crown originates from a cap, turban, or more formal metallic crown decorated with jewels. Historically, when an individual was adorned with a crown, it indicated the person was set apart for specific work. In the Bible, those who wear a crown are honored for eternity.

---

1. Incorruptible crown: 1 Corinthians 9:24-25 (NIV): "Do you not know that in a race all the runners run, but only one gets the prize? Run in such a way as to get the prize. Everyone who competes in the games goes into strict training. They do it to get a crown that will not last; but we do it to get a crown that will last forever."

2. Crown of rejoicing: 1 Thessalonians 2:19-20

3. Crown of life: James 1:12

4. Crown of righteousness: 2 Timothy 4:8

5. Crown of glory: 1 Peter 5:2-4

Assign each group a passage from the handout. Allow about five minutes for groups to work. While kids work, discreetly adhere the adhesive gems to the paper crown template and cut it out. Then place the crown face down near you to show the kids after they explain their discoveries.

Say: **Let's learn from each other about the crowns or rewards in heaven.**

Have willing kids from each group describe what they learned about their crown.

Ask: • **What surprises you about these different crowns?**

• **Why do you think God rewards the things we learned about on the crowns?**

Reveal the crown shape with the gems on it from the opening experience. Let kids pass around the crown as they each answer the following:

Ask: • **What's one thing you can do this week to live for God?**

Say: **Just like people in the Bible gained a reward in heaven for living for God,** **God wants us to live for him, too.**

Have kids put their "Five Crowns" handouts in their Travel Journals, and collect the journals until the end of your session.

ADVENTURES IN GROWING

(15 minutes)
Food for Thought

Children decorate cookies to learn that living for God can be difficult—but worth the reward.

Say: **In a moment, you'll each get a cookie to decorate and eat. But there's a catch. You can only use the items I give you to decorate your cookies.** Hold up a popsicle stick. **You can only put icing on your cookie with a popsicle stick.** Hold up a flat toothpick. **And you can only put on the sprinkles with a toothpick.**

TOUR GUIDE TIP

If you have younger kids, read the Scriptures aloud to the entire group and let kids draw rather than write details about the crowns.

Items to Pack:

undecorated sugar cookies, white icing, a variety of sparkly sprinkles, flat toothpicks (round ones won't work), 1 popsicle stick per child, small plates or napkins

ALLERGY ALERT ▸ Check with parents about allergies and dietary concerns, and post a copy of the "Allergy Alert" sign (at the end of this book) where parents will see it.

You can't use your fingers to pinch sprinkles or ice the cookie, and it has to be decorated before you can eat it. Give each child a popsicle stick, a toothpick, and a sugar cookie on a paper plate or napkin. Have the icing and sprinkles where kids can all reach them. **Ready, go!**

Allow about three minutes for kids to work; then gather their attention back to you. Let kids eat their cookies while you discuss the following.

Ask: • **Explain whether this experience was easy or difficult for you.**

• **Tell whether your cookie reward was worth the bother of decorating it.**

• **How was this experience like or unlike the reward in heaven when we live for God?**

Say: **To get any reward, you have to be willing to do the hard work. Progress might seem slow and sometimes we can wonder if it's worth it. But like just now when you got to eat your cookie, you'll get the reward when you stay focused.**  **God wants us to live for him, even though it can be hard work. When we live for God, he will reward us in heaven. All the hard work will be worth it.**

Ask kids to help clean up.

 **SOUVENIRS →**

(10 minutes)

Taking Flight

Kids discover ways they can live for God.

Distribute pencils and the "Livin' for God" handout.

Say: **We've spent today talking about how**  **God wants us to live for him. Take a moment to silently work on the handout to help you think of ways you can live for God in real life. You'll find some ideas on the page, but please come up with your own, too.** Play some quiet music while kids work, if you like.

Ask: • **What are things we can *do* to live for God?**

• **What are things we can *say* to live for God?**

• **What kinds of things can make it hard to live for God?**

• **What are ways we can overcome the hard things so we stay focused on God?**

Items to Pack:
Bibles, 1 copy per child of the "Livin' for God" handout (at the end of this lesson), pencils, quiet music and music player (optional)

Say: **These are great ideas. Now turn to a partner and decide which one thing you'll focus on doing or saying this week.**

Allow time for conversation. Then gather kids' attention back to you.

HOME AGAIN PRAYER

(up to 5 minutes)

Items to Pack:
the paper crown with gems from the opening prayer experience

Say: **Everyone, please come up one at a time and tear off a piece of our crown that includes a gem, and take it back to where you were sitting. Hold it in your hand.**

Say: ◕ **God wants us to live for him. He wants us to be joyful, even when it's hard, because we can have faith that our reward in heaven will be worth all the hard times. God wants to give us a crown for staying focused on him and living for him. God wants us to help each other live for him, too.**

First I'll pray for you, and then you'll have an opportunity to pray for each other.

Pray: **Dear God, thank you for every person in this room. We know you have created each of us for a special purpose and that we have important things to do here. Please help us remember that even when it's hard, we can always hold onto happiness knowing that you love us and will reward us in heaven. Please be with us during those times when it's hard to stay focused on you. Help us remember to cheer each other on as we live for you.**

Quietly pray for the person on your right. Allow time.

Pray: **God, we're holding a piece of a crown that reminds us that when we serve you, you will reward us. Help us overcome obstacles this week so we can live for you, be good examples and encouragers to our friends, and stay joyful. Thank you for taking us on this journey through all the Beatitudes with each other and you. Thank you for being faithful to us and for loving us. We love you. In Jesus' name, amen.**

Distribute the Travel Journals for kids to take home, and thank kids for joining you on this exciting adventure!

Crown Template

5 CROWNS

Instructions: Look up your assigned passage. Then come up with characteristics related to that crown. You can write or draw examples of the characteristic.

1 Corinthians 9:24-25 (NIV)

1 Thessalonians 2:19-20

James 1:12

2 Timothy 4:8

1 Peter 5:2-4

Livin' FOR God

INSTRUCTIONS: Determine what you can do this week to live for God.

1. What are things you can DO to help you live for God?

2. What are things you can SAY to help you live for God?

3. What can make it hard to live for God?

4. What are ways we can overcome the hard things so we stay focused on God?

5. How can you live for God this week?

Parents, we will be eating a snack in class today.

Please let your child's teacher know if your child has any allergies or dietary concerns.

ALLERGY ALERT!

We're serving...

You'll also love these other Kids' Travel Guides

Kids' Travel Guide to the Parables

The parables of Jesus are rich resources for transforming children! This edition of the *Kids' Travel Guide* series explores 13 of Jesus'"greatest hits" parables. Lead kids (age levels K-5th grade) on a 13-week exploration of the parables that will help them understand what God wants of them. *Kids' Travel Guide to the Parables* includes "Pathway Points" to focus kids in on the point to each parable in fun and interactive ways. It's perfect for Sunday school or midweek, and flexible—works for 2 kids...12 kids...20 kids!

▶ ISBN 978-0-7644-7013-4 • $19.99 *In Canada $22.99*

Kids' Travel Guide to the 23rd Psalm

▶ ISBN 978-0-7644-4005-2
$19.99 *In Canada $22.99*

Kids' Travel Guide to the Fruit of the Spirit

▶ ISBN 978-0-7644-2390-1
$19.99 *In Canada $22.99*

Kids' Travel Guide to the Lord's Prayer

▶ ISBN 978-0-7644-2524-0
$19.99 *In Canada $22.99*

Kids' Travel Guide to the Ten Commandments

▶ ISBN 978-0-7644-2224-9
$19.99 *In Canada $22.99*

Kids' Travel Guide to the Armor of God

▶ ISBN 978-0-7644-2695-7
$19.99 *In Canada $22.99*

Each book includes 13 lessons with these fun features to help take your kids on a travel adventure:

- **In-Focus Verse** around which the adventure is focused.
- **Departure Prayer** designed for children to add their own words of prayer.
- **First-Stop Discoveries:** Narrated enactment or group activity exploring the lesson's Bible story.
- **Story Excursions:** Through Bible stories, bring the book's biblical theme to life in fun, imaginative, and dramatic ways.
- **Adventures in Growing:** Activities show kids how to apply what they've learned to their daily lives!
- **Souvenirs:** Kids create pages that go into a notebook (their very own travel journal!) to remind them of the lesson's Bible point.

Order today! Visit group.com or your favorite Christian retailer.

Tons of fun ways to reinforce Bible points!

The Humongous Book of Games for Children's Ministry

Super-size fun with 220 games that reinforce Bible points. You'll always have a great big fun game at your fingertips for any area of children's ministry. Indexed by Scripture and energy level.

▶ ISBN 978-0-7644-2355-0
$29.99 *In Canada $32.99*

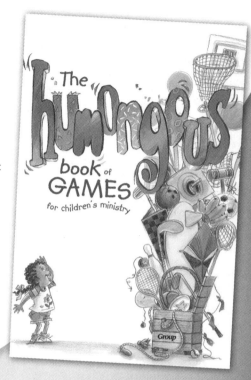

Also available in this series:

The Humongous Book of Bible Skits

▶ ISBN 978-0-7644-3083-1 • $29.99
In Canada $32.99 (BOOK & CD)

The Humongous Book of Children's Messages

▶ ISBN 978-0-7644-2647-6 • $29.99
In Canada $32.99

The Humongous Book of Preschool Ideas

▶ ISBN 978-0-7644-3601-7 • $29.99
In Canada $32.99

The Humongous Book of Preschool Ideas 2

▶ ISBN 978-0-7644-3813-4 • $29.99
In Canada $32.99

Order today! Visit group.com or your favorite Christian retailer.

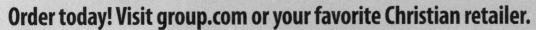

Secret weapons for *getting kids' attention!*

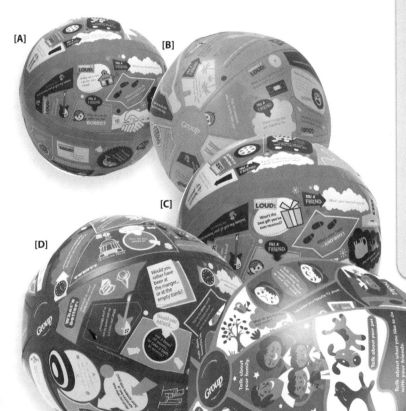